The
EVERYTHING®
Rock & Blues Guitar Book

Dear Reader:

A great deal of thought went into the best way to present the material in this book. In guitar education, emphasis has been placed on licks and learning verbatim lines. While this may be important, I feel that as a student, the best teachers are your favorite players. And while this book could be a collection of licks and phrases, I couldn't possibly do it any better than the guitar masters who have come before. With that in mind, this book is set up to show you what you need to know to play and be a successful student, not just to play licks. This book is about showing you the typical things that come up in guitar playing: chords, scales, and everything else under the sun. Contained within these pages are many lifetimes of information, and if you study it carefully and apply it to real musical situations, you will have great success as a player. The guitar is a complex and personal instrument and every player will do it differently. I have left much of the information up to you the reader so that you can make your own conclusions about music. Study, think, and enjoy.

Marc Schonbrun

The EVERYTHING® Series

Editorial

Publishing Director	Gary M. Krebs
Managing Editor	Kate McBride
Copy Chief	Laura MacLaughlin
Acquisitions Editor	Eric Hall
Development Editor	Karen Johnson Jacot
Production Editor	Khrysti Nazzaro

Production

Production Director	Susan Beale
Production Manager	Michelle Roy Kelly
Series Designers	Daria Perreault
	Colleen Cunningham
Cover Design	Paul Beatrice
	Frank Rivera
Layout and Graphics	Colleen Cunningham
	Rachael Eiben
	Michelle Roy Kelly
	Daria Perreault
	Erin Ring
Cover Artist	Leslie Dunlap
Audio Production	Marc Schonbrun
Music Typesetting	Marc Schonbrun and
	WR Music Service

Visit the entire Everything® Series at everything.com

THE
EVERYTHING®
ROCK & BLUES
GUITAR
BOOK

From chords to scales and licks to
tricks, all you need to play like the greats

Marc Schonbrun

Adams Media Corporation
Avon, Massachusetts

This book is dedicated to the memory of Eric Harrison.

An Everything® Series Book.
Everything® and everything.com® are registered trademarks of F+W Publications, Inc.

Published by Adams Media, an F+W Publications Company
57 Littlefield Street, Avon, MA 02322 U.S.A.
www.adamsmedia.com

ISBN: 1-58062-883-4
Printed in the United States of America.

J I H G F E D C B

Library of Congress Cataloging-in-Publication Data
Schonbrun, Marc.
The everything rock & blues guitar book / Marc Schonbrun.
p.   cm.   (An Everything series book)
ISBN 1-58062-883-4
1. Guitar–Methods–Self-instruction. 2. Guitar–Methods
(Blues) 3. Guitar–Methods (Rock) I. Title. II. Title: Everything
rock and blues guitar book. III. Series: Everything series.
MT588.S357 2003
787.87'193'166—dc21
2003000376

This book is available at quantity discounts for bulk purchases.
For information, call 1-800-872-5627.

Contents

Acknowledgments

Thanks to Mom, Dad, David, Bill, Dr. Rubio, Greg Utzig, Joe Mooney,
Dr. Steinberg, Bret Zvacek, and Mike Riley for recording help.
Extra thanks to my wife, Karla, for her tremendous love and support.

Recording

The CD in this book was recorded at Herkimer Sound, in New York,
using an Apple Macintosh G4 running Digidesign Pro Tools. All sound
was direct to disk using a Parker Fly Deluxe and a '72 Fender Telecaster
Thinline through a Line6 POD Pro. All guitars strung with D'Addario
strings. All tracks played live by Marc Schonbrun.

Top Ten Things
You'll Learn from This Book

1. The pentatonic scale—the five notes you need to know to play rock and blues.

2. Inflection and phrasing—the little slides and bends that dress up a note and give you that unique, signature sound.

3. Major and minor scales—the basic vocabulary of guitar.

4. Basic music theory—a quick and easy introduction to the "language" of music.

5. Chords and chord progressions—understand which notes sound good together and why.

6. Impressive flourishes like tapping and sweep-picking to help you push the envelope of guitar playing.

7. Making the most of slides and capos to give you the unique sound you're looking for.

8. Playing it by ear—training your ear to recognize and play the notes in your head or on the radio.

9. Tools of the trade—from guitars and amps, to effects and pickups, know what you need and how to get it cheap.

10. Practice makes perfect—and a great guitar player. Learn how to make the most of your practice time.

Introduction

▶ WELCOME to *The Everything® Rock & Blues Guitar Book!* You are embarking on quite a journey to learn about two exciting genres, so plug in and hold on. Guitar playing is a vast and open-ended topic. The goal here is to equip students with the material required to advance toward their full potential.

There is no single "right" way to play guitar. In fact, it's the diversity of performers that keeps such a wide audience interested. This book will show you all the important techniques and concepts that make rock and blues guitar what they are.

This book is designed for players who have been playing guitar for a little while. To utilize this book effectively, you should know your basic open-position chords and moveable barre chords at a minimum. Advanced players will find plenty of material to keep their attention. The chapters in this book are organized in a logical order, but you should feel free to skip around. Whether you've played for twenty years or twenty minutes, there is something here for you.

This book covers all aspects of guitar from the most basic blues riff to extravagant and complex two-handed tapping. At first, new concepts and sounds may seem foreign, even unsettling. In time, these will become as familiar as your favorite power chord. You'll be able to see your own progress by revisiting old material. Melodies that are a challenge when you begin will seem easy after a few months of practice using this book as a guide.

A large portion of this book focuses on lead playing. In rock and blues, lead playing is a vital and important concept. In its relatively short life, lead guitar playing has found a permanent place in these styles of music. This book presents you with a logical and organized way to learn lead guitar and apply the concepts and licks to your music.

Throughout this book, musical examples help to illustrate ideas that are discussed in the chapters. All the examples use standard notation and tablature. If you can't read music yet, don't worry. That's covered here too.

By practicing, the musical examples, ideas, and concepts expressed in the text will become clear. The accompanying audio CD will bring the examples from the written page into rich living examples.

The focus of this book is application, not theory. Each chapter consists of new material followed by extensive discussion on where to use the new ideas and concepts. You'll be able to hone your skills and find your own sound with the skills you learn from this book. Let's get started! Ⓔ

E How to Use This Book and CD

To get the most out of this book, we should talk about some of the notation and terms that will be used throughout this text. Some of it you have seen before; some of it may be new to you.

Standard Notation and Tablature

For every example that uses music, there will be a double staff showing a standard five-line music staff with a six-line tab staff below it. The tablature (or tab) staff won't contain rhythms because the music staff contains that information. The tab just indicates on which fret (0 through 24) to play the notes.

Here's an example of what you will see in this book. Every example that uses music will be written this way.

FIGURE 1 Notation and tab example

Neck Diagrams

Neck diagrams are handy when talking about scales. Instead of a written scale in music notation, the neck diagram gives you a general roadmap of which notes can be played for a particular scale. All of the neck diagrams used in this book are for scale shapes. An example of a typical neck diagram is on the facing page.

This diagram is an overhead view of a guitar neck. If you lay the guitar on your lap (strings up) you're looking at the same picture. The lowest string is closest to your body and the highest string is farthest away. Each finger is numbered one through four ("one" is your index finger), so you can see what finger to use. Frets are sometimes numbered above the diagrams, or the correct fret to play may be indicated by a dot on the

FIGURE 2   Neck diagram

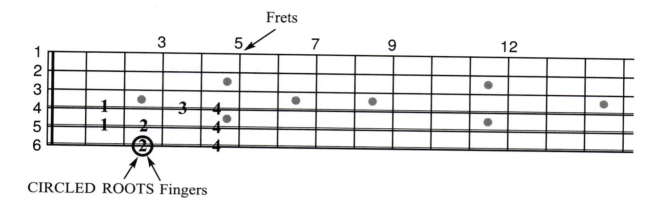

CIRCLED ROOTS Fingers

neck diagram. The root of each scale (that is, the key name of each scale, such as key of A, E, and so on) will always have a circle around the finger number. This type of notation is great for scales because you want to use the whole scale and not get caught up in musical phrasings, also known as licks. By looking at the neck this way, you can learn which notes to play and your creativity will give you the order.

Chord Boxes

Chord boxes are fairly standard, but let's look at an example. Each of the chord boxes will show you a four- or five-fret area of the neck. As you can see from the following diagram, the lowest string is on the left and the highest string is on the right. Place your fingers as shown in the diagram on the appropriate pitches. Unless you see a small number beside the chord diagram, these chords are in the first open position ("open position" refers to chords in the first three frets that involve open strings). If you see a number beside the diagram, it means that the chord shape starts at that fret.

FIGURE 3 Chord box

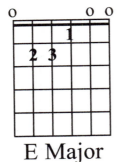

E Major

An "X" above a string means don't play that string. A "O" above a string means to play that string open. Pay careful attention to the Xs and Os when playing the chord shapes.

Audio Examples

TRACK 1

As often as possible, the examples are played on the accompanying audio CD that is included with this book. The examples are played at a moderate speed so you can hear the idea and also practice along with it. In this book, the CD symbol with a track number underneath it corresponds to tracks on the CD. The first track is an introduction and tuning notes so you can play along with the CD. The CD is a great tool that will help you unlock the more difficult examples and get them just right.

Guitar Terminology

Let's curb any confusion before it starts! The lowest string on the guitar is the low E sixth string. It is the string closest to your body. It's the lowest string because it sounds the lowest, not because of the geographical location on the instrument. The lowest string is called the sixth string, and the strings are named from six to one, stopping at the high E string, which is the thinnest string, closest to the floor. E

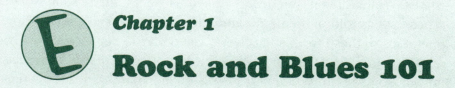

Chapter 1

Rock and Blues 101

How did we get here? What are the roots of rock and blues music and how did they play off of each other? Here is a brief history of the two styles and how guitar has become a permanent fixture in modern music, especially lead guitar.

The Origins of the Blues

The blues has its roots in Africa. Many of the rhythms used in the blues, especially the swing rhythms, are ancient tribal rhythms. The rhythmic influence was passed on through African-Americans whose ancestors had left their home in Africa, either by their own will or, more commonly, as slaves. While African-Americans worked as slaves, many sang work songs. These songs told of their pain and plight as oppressed slaves. The melodies of these work songs were based on the pentatonic (five tones)/ blues scale, rather than the seven-tone major scale that Western classical music is based on. When slavery was ended, many African-Americans stayed in the South while others headed north. As a result, the blues is usually divided into two main categories: southern and northern blues. The evolution of the slave songs spilled into the church and gospel music. During church services in the South, gospel music played a major role. During the songs, one or more soloists would improvise flourishes based on the pre-existing melody of spiritual and hymn songs. This is where improvisation was born. Many singers based their melodies solely on the pentatonic scale. Many of the spiritual songs were based on repeating chord progressions of simple chords.

The church was not the only place that gave birth to blues music. In the late 1800s, street vendors would sometimes "call" their products out by singing about them. Often, the melody was based on the pentatonic scale. On some of the historic recordings of street vendors, you can play the twelve-bar blues progressions behind the "calls" and it fits together. During those years, the combination of pentatonic melodies and basic chord progressions were starting to fuse into what would become known as the blues.

ESSENTIAL

For a more detailed look at the history of the guitar and its players, *The Everything® Guitar Book,* by Jack Wilkins and Peter Rubie, is a wonderful reference for history and beginning to play in general. Check it out.

Blues Styles, Artists, and Evolution

There is no precise moment when the blues started, and different regions developed their own blues styles over time. Although blues styles differed from region to region, one thing was the same in each variation of the blues: the scales and chords were similar. As blues progressed, it was passed down in an aural tradition from player to player (there was no "music conservatory" for the blues). Many players simply learned it from other players. Each style of blues relied heavily on singers, and some of the earliest recorded blues performances were of singers accompanied either by guitar, banjo, or piano.

The ability to travel almost anywhere in the country by railway and the advent of the automobile industry made it easier than ever for people to move between regions, hearing new sounds and bringing their own styles with them. The technology that made recordings possible gave blues the opportunity to reach every corner of America.

FACT

There are too many important blues players to mention them all, but some worth checking out are Blind Lemon Jefferson, Howlin' Wolf, Robert Johnson, Lonnie Johnson, and B.B. King.

The Guitar's Role

The role of the guitar in early blues music was to accompany singers. A guitar was a cheap and readily available alternative to a piano. Some of the earliest Robert Johnson recordings featured only solo voice with guitar accompaniment. For live performances, the piano was the preferred accompaniment instrument because it was able to project much louder than the acoustic guitar. The solo instruments of the blues were harmonica, voice, saxophone, and, occasionally, trumpet and clarinet. Because of the volume problems inherent in the acoustic guitar, it never caught on as a strong solo instrument. But the popularity of guitar was immense and acoustic jams were frequent in the churches and halls of the Deep South.

The invention of the electric guitar changed the role of guitar forever. Finally, the guitar was capable of carrying a band as an accompanist and a suitably loud soloist. The blues now had a solo instrument and rhythm player all in one, and the popularity of the electric guitar and electric blues exploded. The electric guitar also gave birth to rock and roll.

The Birth of Rock

Rock and roll started simply as an offshoot of blues. Early rock and roll was nothing more than amplified blues progressions with a harder edge. But the influence from blues was undeniable; many of the same chord progressions and song forms were used. For the soloist, the scale of choice was still the pentatonic scale. As rock and roll progressed in the 1950s, the guitar's place as a lead instrument was starting to solidify.

Until the introduction of the electric guitar, the saxophone had been the instrument of choice for soloing because of its loud and powerful tone. But the electric guitar began to replace the sax as the lead instrument in the 1950s and 1960s.

The birth of rock and roll spelled the end for the saxophone in rock music. The sax would find favor in R&B and jazz. With each passing year, rock developed its own identity and started to sound less and less like the blues.

Rock Evolution

Rock music grew from the blues, but quickly evolved in every direction. The 1950s gave us the music of Elvis Presley and Buddy Holly. In the 1960s, the British invasion brought us The Beatles and the Rolling Stones who both helped to shape the sound of rock and legitimize rock as "real" music, based on blues roots but also borrowing from the European-classical tradition. The 1960s saw explosive change and the entrance of the most important guitarist in the history of rock and roll: Jimi Hendrix.

Hendrix, in one fell swoop, changed the guitar and rock music forever. His style was largely based on blues, but with a harder edge. He was experimental and most people consider him the father of distortion and effects. Hendrix changed the tone of the instrument from soft and twangy to loud and explosive. The 1970s were a rough era—guitar music took a backseat to disco. Disco was king, but that didn't stop innovative bands like the Eagles, the Who, and Pink Floyd from producing breakthrough albums that pushed the envelope.

The 1980s saw important changes in the technique used to play the instrument. Virtuosos such as Yngwie Malmsteen, Steve Vai, and Joe Satriani pushed the instrument to places it had never been before. The decade of the 1980s was also the age of the guitar solo. In no previous time had technique and guitar soloing been so important.

The 1990s saw the death of "hair-metal" and the birth of grunge. Bands like Nirvana, Pearl Jam, and Soundgarden pioneered the "Seattle" sound, which featured songwriting over virtuosity. The 1990s were a subdued time for guitar and guitar playing—a reaction to all the excess of the 1980s. And rock music continues to evolve today.

Teaching Lead Guitar

There needs to be a separation of what you can and can't teach in a book like this. The blues is based on a standard repeating chord progression and because of this, we can talk about the rhythms and chords of the blues. However, rock music has no standards. Each artist does something unique, so trying to quantify it is difficult. As a result, many players learn to play rock guitar by learning a multitude of songs and being creative. Still, there's one aspect that you can teach and discuss, and that's lead guitar.

Lead guitar is an important part of playing guitar, especially in rock and blues music, but it's a huge and mysterious topic to some. Many players have little or no problem playing chords and rhythm guitar, but when it comes to playing lead or playing solos, many are puzzled about what to do. Fortunately, the elements of lead guitar can be taught in an organized way. Unlike chords and songwriting, which can be put together in an infinite variety, the elements that make up leads and lead playing (scales, arpeggios, modes) are self contained and important to discuss. This book, while it will spend time on chords and chord progressions, will spend a great deal of time talking about the elements that make lead what it is. Guitar, in rock and blues, functions largely as a lead instrument, and for many, playing a better lead guitar remains a perplexing mystery. We will set out here, chapter by chapter, to show you how music is put together and how it can be applied to lead. So turn to the next page and we can start talking about the basics. E

Chapter 2

Rock and
Blues Styles

Guitar players have long had a fascination with the blues. It's hard to find a rock player who isn't influenced by it. Blues music is based on repeating patterns of chords that have remained unchanged since the birth of the blues. Rock music is built on that foundation and has added traits all its own.

Open-Position Chords

There are several things you need to know and understand to successfully play rock and blues style. For many players, chord- and rhythm-playing is a good place to begin. Most students begin with a few open-position chords and move toward lead-playing as they get more comfortable. Since rhythm-playing is a great place to begin, let's discuss the open-position chords in detail.

Open-position chords are chords that use the first four frets of the guitar in their formations. The term "open" is used because the chord is partly composed of open strings, meaning strings that your fingers don't press. **FIGURE 2-1** shows you the most common open-position chords played in rock and blues music.

FIGURE 2-1   Important open-position chords

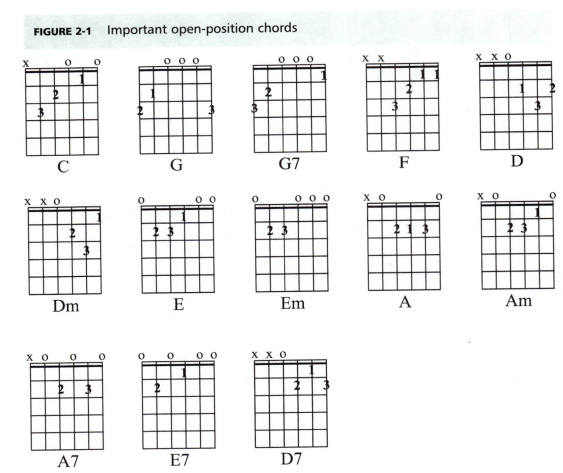

To really say that you know these chords, you have to be able to move from chord to chord with ease. You must memorize them because they are used in virtually every song you come across. Certain chord shifts can be very difficult to hit at first. Many students find the F chord a real problem—it's a tough chord—but the importance of chord-playing can't be overlooked. Until you can play the chords to your favorite song, you'll probably want to shy away from the solos for now. Rhythm-playing makes up about 95 percent of a guitar player's role; the other 5 percent is spent on solos. Spend as much time as you need on the chords to give yourself a good grounding.

The open-position chords are very common in rock and blues rhythm playing. There's a simple reason for this: open-position chords are easier to play. Open strings are like "free fingers" and allow us to play notes without fingering them. It can be strenuous to hold down all your fingers

FIGURE 2-2 Open-position chord progression examples

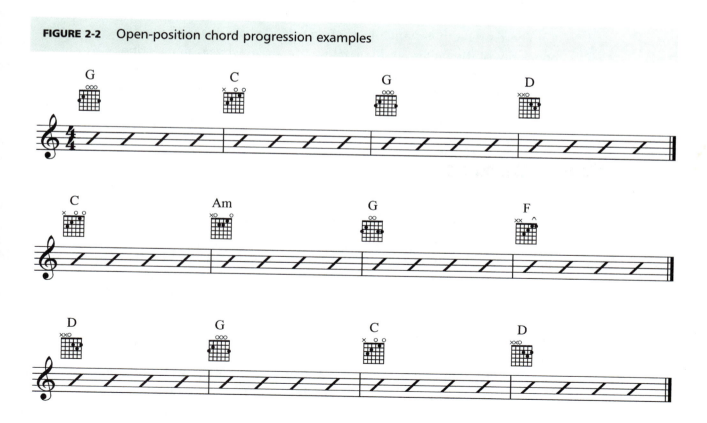

at once, and open strings give your fingers a break. Open-position chords tend to have five or six notes in them and have a larger range than other chords found on the guitar, which are normally, but not exclusively, limited to four notes—one per finger.

In **FIGURE 2-2** are some examples of very common open-position chord progressions you may find in your favorite songs. Try to shift smoothly and evenly between the chords while you play.

The limiting factor of open-position chords lies in the open strings themselves. Only chords that contain the open strings are possible. What if you want to play a B flat chord? A "B flat" chord doesn't have any open position; because the open strings don't work with that chord (more on this in Chapter 8). The same is true of many other chords, so you can see the open position won't help you gain full use of the guitar's chordal ability. The guitar is capable of playing wonderful and beautiful-sounding chords; but you will need to learn more than the open-position chords to get the full range of possibilities.

There aren't that many different chords. Couple this with the popularity of the guitar, and you can understand why so many songs sound similar: Many songs are based on exactly the same chords, just in a different order. The guitar's open position is limited; it takes a good player to get to the next step.

Barre Chords

In order to play all the possible chords on the guitar, you must learn the concept of moveable chords. A moveable chord has a finger pattern than can be moved around the guitar without altering the shape of the chord. To achieve this, the guitar uses barre chords. The concept of a barre is very simple; one finger lies flat across the guitar neck and plays multiple notes. Look at **FIGURE 2-3** to see what a G-Major barre chord looks like.

All of the notes that are played on the third fret are played with the first (index) finger. The finger lays flat across all the strings and clamps them down—this is what barre chords all do. Barre chords are difficult and require a lot of practice. It's normal to have trouble with them at first—keep practicing and you will get them. Barre chords enable you to play a five- or six-note chord with only four fingers. Without barre chords, guitar chords would be limited to only four notes—one per finger.

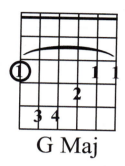

FIGURE 2-3
G-Major
barre chord

G Maj

The beauty of barre chords is that they're moveable, meaning you can use the same shape as in **FIGURE 2-3** and move it to another fret staying on the same string and change the name of the chord—without changing the fingering. This simplifies chords for guitar players. Instead of having to learn a different shape for each chord as in the open position, you can maintain the basic shapes and just move them to different frets.

As a rock and blues guitar player, the most common chords you deal with are major chords and minor chords. If you can play any major and minor chord on the guitar, there will be little you can't play as a rhythm player. There are four different barre chord shapes to learn on the guitar to accomplish this task. There are two major barre chord forms, one on the sixth string, one on the fifth; and two minor barre chord forms, also on the sixth and fifth strings. The two forms result because the roots are placed on the sixth and fifth strings. Each string yields its own shape. **FIGURE 2-4** is an example of the four different barre chord shapes broken down by string.

FIGURE 2-4
Moveable
barre
shapes

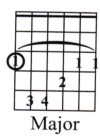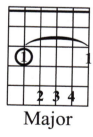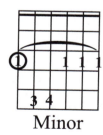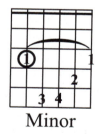

Major   Major   Minor   Minor

To be able to move a chord, you have to know how chords get their names. All chords are named from the lowest note in the chord. With the moveable chord forms in **FIGURE 2-4**, the lowest note falls on either the sixth string or the fifth string. To move the chords, all you have to know is the name of the notes on the low strings. Then you can move the barre chord shapes to the appropriate location and play any chord

FIGURE 2-5 String charts for E and A strings

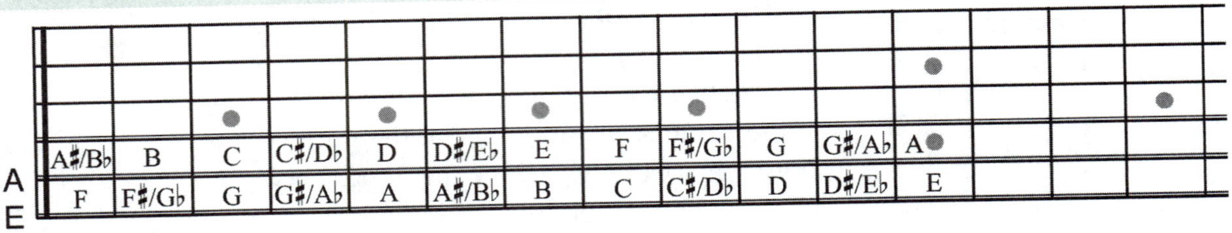

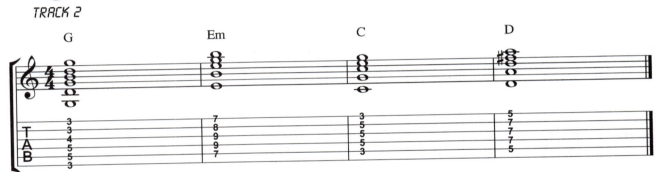

A♯/B♭	B	C	C♯/D♭	D	D♯/E♭	E	F	F♯/G♭	G	G♯/A♭	A●
F	F♯/G♭	G	G♯/A♭	A	A♯/B♭	B	C	C♯/D♭	D	D♯/E♭	E

A
E

FIGURE 2-6 Standard rock chord progression

TRACK 2

you want. **FIGURE 2-5** is a chart to help you find the chord names for moveable barre shapes.

Now that you have the concept down, let's apply this to a piece of music. **FIGURE 2-6** uses barre chords in a standard rock chord progression.

This example uses the same barre chord shapes from **FIGURE 2-4** and applies them to some different chords. For a barre chord to work, you have to apply even pressure across the guitar neck. Otherwise, some strings will sound muted.

Reading Chord Charts

Once you've mastered the open-position chords and the moveable barre chords, you're ready to play almost anything that comes your way. Unlike music for the piano, guitar sheet music typically doesn't use standard notation for its chord playing. The ability to read standard notation is extremely important to being a good, well rounded musician. As a guitarist, reading chord charts is a more common part of the job. Typically a chord chart consists of two elements: chord name and duration. Most chord charts won't show you exactly how to play the chords; you're expected to be able to play basic major and minor chords. Some charts will show a small chord box (like the ones in **FIGURE 2-2**) to aid you in playing the correct chord voicing.

Voicing refers to the way a chord is played. A simple C-Major chord can be played many different ways on the guitar; each is a different voicing. For example an open C-Major chord and an 8th fret barre chord are considered two different voicings of the same chord. If a guitar player is supposed to use an unusual chord voicing in place of a open chord, the chord charts will specify exactly how to play that chord.

The duration of the chord will be expressed in slash notation—one slash equals one strike of a chord with your pick or fingers. This simple

FIGURE 2-7   Open position D and A chords with chord chart

FIGURE 2-8   D and A chords using barre chords

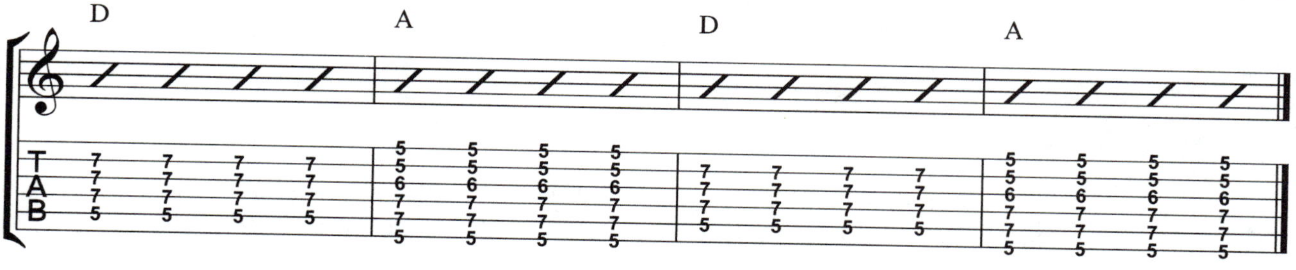

way of notating guitar chords is common and acceptable. Chord charts are also used in jazz, country, blues, and commercial music styles. Many players find it faster to read the chord symbol C Major than to read the standard notation for the chord.

FIGURE 2-7 is a simple chord chart showing a D-Major chord followed by an A-Major chord using open-position chords.

When you read this chord chart you can play any version of a D-Major chord you wish—either the open position D or a D-Major barre chord are fine.

FIGURE 2-8 shows how the barre chords would substitute for the open chords.

Notice the difference in sound between the open-position chords and the barre chords. Play both examples again to compare the different chords. The choice of which to use depends on your personal preference.

Standard Sheet Music

If you've ever looked at the sheet music to your favorite song, you probably noticed that standard sheet music usually doesn't include guitar tablature. The only thing you'll find pertaining to the guitar are the chord boxes above the music. The chord boxes serve as a general suggestion of what you can play along with the song. Music publishers that include guitar chord boxes are not supplying the guitar parts exactly as played by your favorite artists. The chord boxes allow you to get the gist of how to play the song; but usually not exactly as the guitarist played it. Chord boxes typically rely on simple open-position chords. For exact versions of your songs, make sure the music includes guitar tablature and music staves. Look for versions that say "recorded guitar parts" printed on the sheet.

Power Chords

Power chords are an integral part of rock and blues guitar playing. After learning open-position and barre chords, mastering power chords is the next important step toward becoming a great rock and blues rhythm player. No one knows where the name "power chord" comes from; but try playing one with a loud amp and you'll get an idea of why "power" is so fitting. Power chords are like barre chords because they are both movable chord shapes. Once you know the shape for a power chord, all you have to do is slide it around the guitar to make riffs. **FIGURE 2-9** shows a power chord shape on the low E string and low A string.

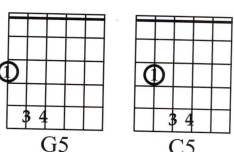

FIGURE 2-9 Power chords

Notice how the shape is the same on both strings. This makes power chords very easy to move around, you end up locking your fingers into that shape and sliding your hand around the neck.

Power chords are commonly found on the low E and low A strings. Since they only use three fingers, and don't have the complexity of barre chords, power chords can be moved around the guitar with ease. Power chord names follow the same rule other chords follow—the lowest note names the chord. In a power chord the lowest note will always fall on your first finger. Power chords are also called fifth chords. The standard symbol for a C power chord is C5. This type of notation helps distinguish it from the standard major and minor chord symbols. Power chords are neither major nor minor; they are in a category all their own.

Some well-known songs that include power chords are:

- "Smells Like Teen Spirit" (Nirvana)
- "Welcome to Paradise" (Green Day)
- "Stairway to Heaven" before the solo (Led Zeppelin)
- "Purple Haze" (Jimi Hendrix)
- "Ironman" (Black Sabbath)

Once you feel comfortable, it's time to start applying power chords to music. Try to play as many of your favorite songs as you can with power chords. By playing guitar parts, you will gain a lot of insight into how guitar parts are created.

Playing the Blues

The blues is very important to guitar players. The blues represents a genre of music, a style of music, and a set of repeating chords common to it. Historically the blues has served as a common meeting point for all players, regardless of style and level. No other style of music uses the same chords in every song like blues does. If you learn what those chords are, you can play blues with anyone.

Twelve Bars

The blues is based on a repeated chord progression that repeats every twelve bars. While no two blues performances will sound the same, the chord progressions and form are always the same. Anyone who knows the twelve-bar blues progressions can sit and play the blues with anyone else.

Because blues is based on a common progression, it's easy to collaborate and play with other blues musicians. It's like an international language of guitar music. You could walk into a blues club anywhere in the world and call "Blue in A," and the players would know exactly what to do. Even if your best friend likes slow Chicago blues, and you like Texas blues, the form and chords are the same, and you can sit down and jam with your friend. You'll be hard-pressed to find someone who doesn't know the blues progression in at least one key. **FIGURE 2-10** shows the twelve-bar blues progression in the key of G.

On chord charts, if the same chord is repeated for a long time, the chord is written only once. You just keep playing that chord until you're told to change.

This pattern repeats over and over again, looping endlessly. **FIGURE 2-11** shows a simple twelve-bar blues pattern, again in the key of G; but instead of open chords, a common rhythm pattern is used. This pattern has been used in countless numbers of blues songs.

This rhythm pattern, which is reminiscent of a power chord with an extra note, is an extremely common way to play blues rhythm guitar. Notice how the original progression is on the top staff and the bottom staff contains another way to play these chords. The basic chords for a G blues progression will never change. However, as your chord options grow you will be able to play more colorful voicings. We see in **FIGURE 2-10** three different ways to play G blues, but the progression hasn't changed; only the way we play the G, C, and D chords.

FIGURE 2-10   Twelve-bar blues in G

TRACK 3

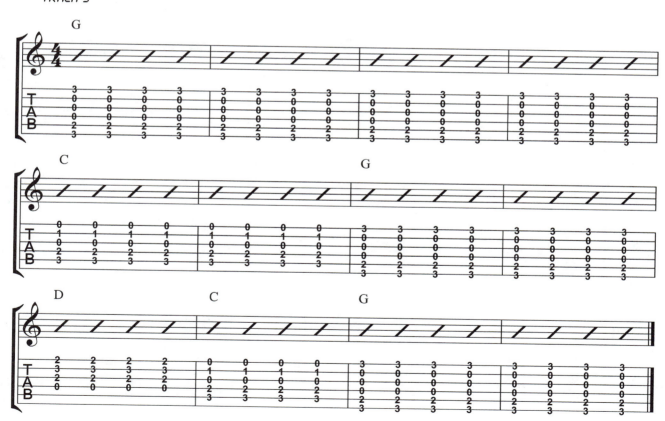

Blues Keys

The twelve-bar blues example in **FIGURE 2-10** contained the chords G, C, and D. Knowing the names of these chords is extremely important and can help you immensely when you play in the key of G. But what happens if you want to play in the key of A, or B♭? When you play the blues, the key is always called as part of the title. A fellow player may say, "Let's play blues in A." So what do you do? How do you know the correct chords for blues in A? Here's where we get into some basic music theory.

 FIGURE 2-11   Shuffle pattern

TRACK 4

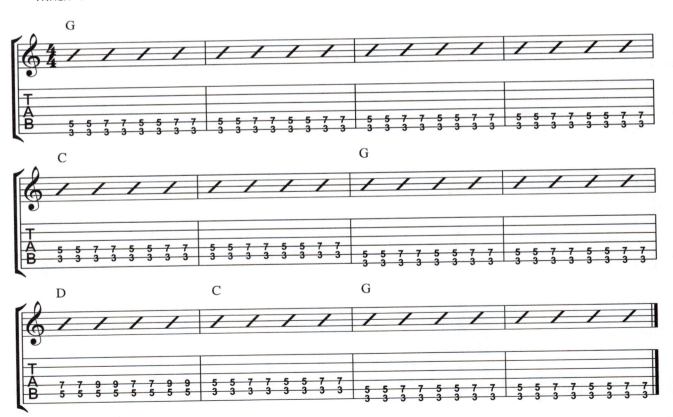

Blues Theory

The musical alphabet uses only seven letter names. A, B, C, D, E, F, and G are the only pitches you'll find. After you get to G, the cycle repeats, starting again at A. This is vital to understanding music theory.

The blues follows a strict regimen of chords. If you play the blues in G, you will play a G, C, and D chord. It will never change; these are the fundamental chords in that key. If you want to move or transpose the chords into a different key, knowing the names of the chords in the G key doesn't really help you very much. Music theory can help you turn a chord

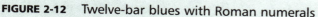

FIGURE 2-12 Twelve-bar blues with Roman numerals

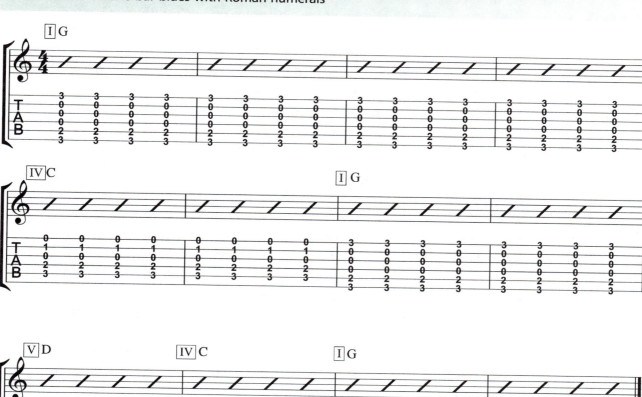

into something that can be played in every key. How? With numbers. Why numbers? Because numbers refer to every key, while pitches and note names are specific to one key. So how will these numbers help us? Let's look at the example of the twelve-bar blues in G again. This time, in addition to the chord symbols, you will see a corresponding number for each chord. Look at the example in **FIGURE 2-12**.

Music theory uses Roman numerals, rather than Arabic numbers. You'll notice that the first chord gets the number I. The chord that shares the same note as the key is always I. For example, in the key of G, a G chord is always I. We give it the number I because it's the first chord we deal with. The C chord has the number IV. Why IV? Well if you count the note G as I, how far up is the note C? (When you count letters in music theory, you always count the first note, don't skip it!) So G is I, A is II, B is III, and C is IV. That's why we call the C chord a IV chord. The root (name of the key) of that chord is four notes away from G. When you're in any key the I chord is considered the center; all the other chords are measured away from I. Using the same logic, the D chord is five away from G, so it is called a V chord.

Applying Theory to Your Playing

Let's turn this from music theory to music reality and apply the concept of numbered chords to playing those chords. These numbers make changing the key easy. Let's apply this to the twelve-bar blues. **FIGURE 2-13** shows the same old trusty twelve-bar blues pattern, but instead of chord names, there are only numbers.

If you would like to play this in the key of A, simply play an A chord each time a I chord is indicated. The other two chords are IV and V. To find those, just count up the musical alphabet starting on A, and count up to get the chords. You should have found D as the IV chord and E as the V chord. Go ahead and plug them into the progression and play. Voilà! You have the blues in A. You can use either open chords or barre chords for the A, D, and E chords.

Does this work with every key? Yes, that's the beauty of music theory. It doesn't talk about specific chords, only the relationships between the chords. In the blues, the form and chord progressions are always the

FIGURE 2-13   Twelve-bar blues pattern with Roman numerals

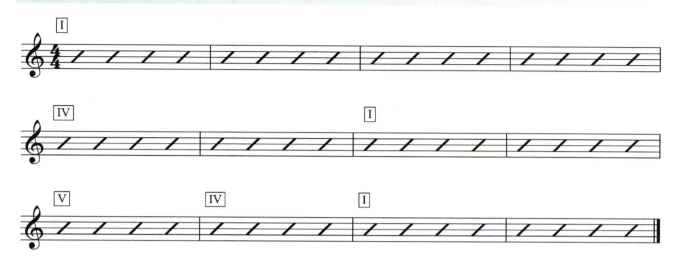

same. Using some theory, some brainpower, and five fingers on your hand to count with, you can now figure out how to play blues in any key. Try playing blues in the key of C using this same technique as practice. I is C, IV is F, and V is G. Try some other keys on your own.

Moveable Theory

The guitar is so well designed that it makes changing keys even easier than using theory. That's right, no counting or thinking involved! The guitar is unique this way—no other instrument works quite like it. Look at **FIGURE 2-14**, a twelve-bar blues progression with moveable barre chords on the low E and A strings.

Notice how the root of the G chord is the third fret, and the root of the C chord is the third fret of the string above? Lets not call the chords G and C, lets call them I and IV as theory tells us to. So if you have a I chord on the low E string, it doesn't matter what fret, the IV chord will be on the same fret just one string up. For example, in the key of A, if your I chord was on the fifth fret of the low E string, than the IV chord will be on the same fret, the fifth, just up one on the A string. Look at **FIGURE 2-15**.

This works in any key! No more counting, just move your chord up one string and you have an instant way to find the IV chord from the I chord.

We can do the same thing for V. The V chord is always two frets above the IV chord. So if the IV chord is on the fifth fret A string, then the V chord is on the seventh fret A string. This makes life so easy. You can simply apply this rule to the blues progression. Pick a key—any key—and start that chord on the low E string. To get a IV chord just move the

FIGURE 2-14   Twelve-bar blues in G with moveable barre chords

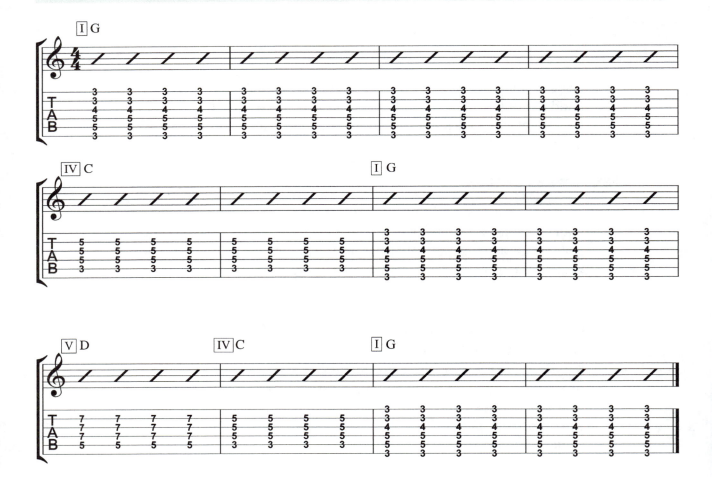

chord up one string. The V chord is two frets above that. You can easily apply this to the previous blues shuffle pattern, **FIGURE 2-11**. This example uses a moveable chord shape. You can move it the same way you move the chords. Let's pick a random key to do this in. How about D♭? D♭ is found on the ninth fret of the low E string. Place your moveable shape on the ninth fret, instant I chord. To get a IV chord, move the shape up one string, and stay on the same fret. To get a V chord, go up two frets from the IV chord to the eleventh fret and place your V chord there. **FIGURE 2-16** shows the blues shuffle pattern in D♭.

FIGURE 2-15   Blues in A

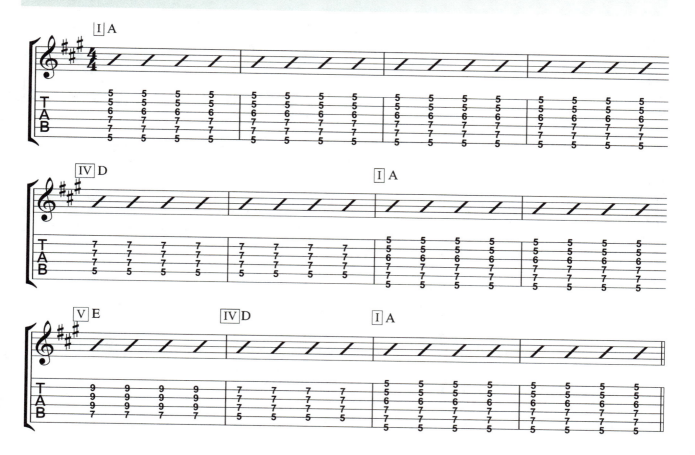

FIGURE 2-16 Blues shuffle in D♭

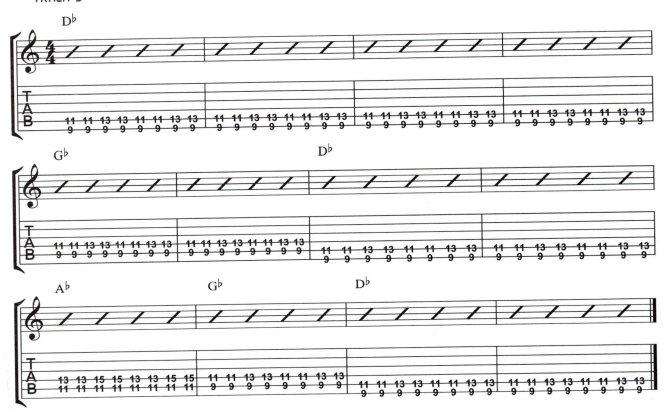

TRACK 5

You can now figure out the locations for any I, IV, and V chord! As long as you follow the order set forth in the twelve-bar blues progression, you can now play blues in any key.

The I-IV-V progression is used in many songs, not just blues. You'll be amazed at how many songs you already know that use this progression. 🄴

Chapter 3

The Pentatonic Scale

The name pentatonic comes from two Greek words: "penta" meaning "five," and "tonic" meaning "notes." Literally, pentatonic means a five-note scale. The pentatonic scale is a staple of rock and blues music; it's used for melodies and as a general vocabulary for improvising. Chances are, if you hear another guitar player soloing, he or she is using the pentatonic scale.

The Most Common Scale

The pentatonic scale, which is commonly called the pentatonic "box," is the most frequently used of all lead scales, and is an absolutely universal tool for playing lead in any style. As a lead player, you need to explore this avenue first. **FIGURE 3-1** is an example of a pentatonic scale in the key of A.

You can see from the music there are only five notes, and they repeat in the same sequence. As you play it try to visualize the shape your fingers make on the fret board. It's essential to memorize the pattern up and down, because this scale will be your main lead scale.

The example in **FIGURE 3-2** is the same scale shape with the note names (pitches) written beneath. Now you can track which five notes make up the scale, and how they repeat.

FIGURE 3-1   A-minor pentatonic scale played up and down

TRACK 6

FIGURE 3-2   A-minor pentatonic scales with pitches identified

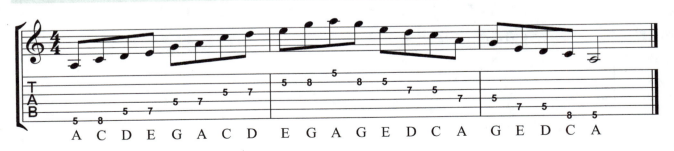

A C D E G A C D E G A G E D C A G E D C A

Learning to Play the Scale

First try to play the scale from bottom to top with no variation. Maybe your first attempt sounded like the example in **FIGURE 3-3**, which is a simple pentatonic scale with no variation in the order of the notes.

It's important to think of the individual notes in the scale as colors on a painter's palette; you can pick and choose any color you wish. In the same way, all the notes in the pentatonic scale are yours for the taking. You can start anyplace you want to, and you can jump to any note in the scale.

The pentatonic scale is so widely played that every guitar player in the world knows it, and everyone will play it a little bit differently. The art of playing this scale lies in your creativity and your approach to making music. Here are a few examples of ways to break up the scale into different combinations. **FIGURE 3-4** is an example of an A-minor pentatonic scale, but the order of the notes has been juggled around.

FIGURE 3-3   Basic pentatonic scale with no variation

FIGURE 3-4   A-minor pentatonic scale with variation on note order

FIGURE 3-5 includes string skipping. Instead of playing it up and down, you can skip from string to string. Remember that you can start and stop anyplace you feel like.

Another example (see **FIGURE 3-6**) of the pentatonic scale, this time you descend the scale from the top and vary the note order.

These examples can serve as a springboard for you to construct your own licks and lines. When you play the scale, try to construct your own original ideas.

In Motion

Now that you have the basic scale shape under your fingers, you may be wondering how to apply this scale to the music you already know. All of the previous examples have been in the key of A. In the pentatonic scale, you derive the key name from the first note you play. The first note of **FIGURE 3-1** is the fifth fret of the low E string. The note on the fifth fret

FIGURE 3-5   A-minor pentatonic scale with string skipping

FIGURE 3-6   A-minor pentatonic scale descending, with variation on note order

is A. It's called an A pentatonic scale, because its key name, also called the root, is A.

So what happens if you're at a jam with some players and they want to play in the key of E? The beauty of the pentatonic scale is that it's moveable. The shape stays the same but if you alter the placement of it, you can easily change the key. **FIGURE 3-7** shows the names of the notes across the low E string to aid you in playing the pentatonic scale in any key.

Using **FIGURE 3-7** you can find out where all the notes are on the low E string. The chart shows you that E is on the twelfth fret. To play the pentatonic scale in E, just shift your box shape up to the twelfth fret and start the scale there. Look at the example in **FIGURE 3-8**—the E pentatonic scale.

One of the special features of the guitar is its ability to let you play in different keys easily. Most other instruments don't give players access to moveable patterns as the guitar does. If you played along as I showed you

FIGURE 3-7   Pitches on the low E string

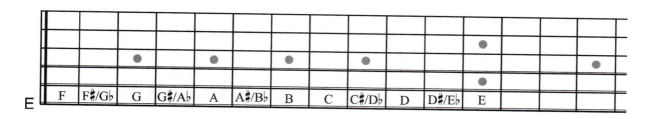

FIGURE 3-8   Pentatonic scale moved to E on the twelfth fret

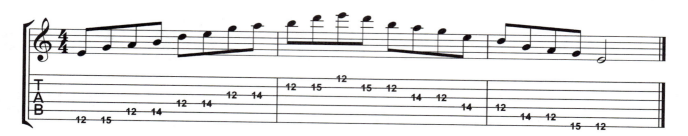

the pentatonic scale, you can already play it in all twelve keys. This feat can take many *months* on other instruments.

Essential Keys

Certain styles of music utilize some keys more than others. Blues is largely played in the keys of A and E, and A is largely considered the "king" of blues keys. Many rock songs are played in the keys of E and G. As you begin to play more lead, you'll become very aware of what key the songs are written in. After awhile, you'll notice that a lot of your favorite bands and guitar players use certain keys more than others.

Do you really play in the key of C♯ often? Not really. The guitar, due to its tuning, tends to produce a great number of songs in the keys of E, A, C, G, and D. Therefore, these are the best keys to practice with.

How do you know what key you're playing in? The name of the key usually comes from a chord or note that is the basis for a song. Many times the key is the first or last chord in a song. (This works most of the time, but not all the time.)

FIGURE 3-9 contains two chords: C and G7. Play through this example and listen very carefully to these two simple chords.

These two chords are in the key of C. How can you tell? After you play the example on the C-Major chord from the beginning, try starting on the G7 chord and stopping there. Just play the G7 chord. Ask yourself this: If that was the last chord in my song, could I just stop? Can you end the song there? No. When you listen to that chord by itself it has a quality that makes it slightly unstable—it wants to go somewhere. Now play the last chord of C. Notice how the example sounds complete?

FIGURE 3-9
C and G7
chords

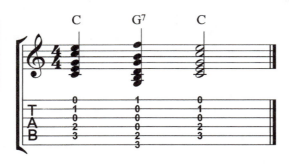

You've just received your best introduction to key. Since C was the chord that you ended on and seemed more "settled," then you are in the key of C. Figuring out what key you're in relies totally on your ear.

In any song, the chord that seems to be most stable is most likely the name of the key. For example, if you believe that the A-minor chord in "Stairway to Heaven" by Led Zeppelin is the correct root chord, then that would be a good guess for the overall key, A minor. You can now test your theory. Try playing the A pentatonic scale during the solo section. Sounds good? Jimmy Page thought so, too; the solo utilizes an A pentatonic scale. Many fans of rock and roll consider "Stairway to Heaven" by Led Zeppelin not only a quintessential rock anthem, but also an important steppingstone in learning to play the guitar. Jimmy Page's solo is also considered a work of art in its simplicity and effectiveness.

Major and Minor Pentatonic Scales

Just as chords come in two versions—major and minor—so do scales. The pentatonic scale you've been using is actually a minor pentatonic scale, and it's the most common for rock and blues music. But many rock bands, such as The Beatles, the Allman Brothers Band, the Grateful Dead, and Phish make use of the major pentatonic scale in their music.

The major pentatonic scale differs from the minor pentatonic scale in only one important way: You start on a different note. The major pentatonic scale starts on the second note and calls that note its root. **FIGURE 3-10** shows a C-Major pentatonic scale.

FIGURE 3-10   C-Major pentatonic scale

TRACK 7

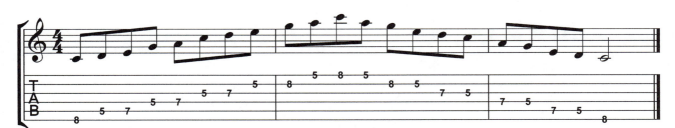

Notice how all the minor pentatonic examples start with the first finger on the low E string, but all the major pentatonic scales begin with the fourth finger on the low E string. Visualizing the scales as shapes can help you learn them quicker.

You might be a bit confused now. How can the minor pentatonic scale use the same basic shape as the major pentatonic? Did you play it yet? If not try it now. Sounds totally different, right? It's an amazing little thing you've just discovered. All you did was change the starting note and the whole sound of the scale changed. This is a crucial concept in music and one you will return to throughout this book.

Music is very economical; it uses only twelve different pitches. Re-using those pitches in a new order yields more variation. Scales often have immensely different sounds if they're played from different starting notes. What's important now is how the scales are different and where we can use them.

Scale Settings

Utilizing the basic shape, you know the only difference between major and minor pentatonic, other than its sound, is what finger you think of as the root. The minor pentatonic uses the first finger on the low E string for its root. The major pentatonic uses the fourth finger as its root. The basic shape stays the same but the name of the scale changes depending on what finger you start on.

So we can now refer to the A-minor pentatonic scale as possibly being a C-Major pentatonic scale. This duality is referred to as a scale relation. Scale relations are discussed in greater detail in Chapter 7. For now, just understand that there is an important connection between A minor and C Major.

Use It or Lose It

Now that you have two scales under your belt, it's important to discuss when and where to use them effectively. If you know the key of the song you're playing, you're in very good shape. A song in the key of A minor uses the A-minor pentatonic scale. A song in the key of G Major uses the G-Major pentatonic scale.

Sometimes you'll run into situations where you don't know which scale to use. Many rock songs utilize power chords for their chordal rhythm playing. Power chords are neither major nor minor, and they actually contain only two notes. Major and minor chords always contain at least three.

When you play power chord–based songs, it can be hard to decide whether to use major or minor pentatonic scales. **FIGURE 3-11** shows three different versions of a C chord: C Major, C minor, and C power (also called C5). Notice how the C power chord sounds neutral compared to the other major and minor chords. Power chords, because they contain fewer notes than major and minor chords, will never sound as rich as major and minor chords that contain three or more notes.

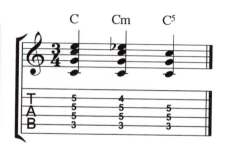

FIGURE 3-11
C-Major, C-minor, and C-power chords

Since power chords don't provide you with a positive answer to whether minor or major pentatonic scales are appropriate, the best way is to experiment with both scales. Try this: Record yourself playing the chords that you'll be soloing over; then try playing both pentatonic scales over the tape to see what sounds best. Your ear will be the ultimate guide as to what sounds good and what doesn't.

For example, if your song ends with an E power chord and you're sure that E is the root, you can try playing an E-Major or an E-minor chord in its place to determine which pentatonic scale to use. Once you have determined which chord sounds correct, you can then play the correct scale. See, this isn't so hard!

Blues Norms

The blues, as a genre, relies almost 99 percent on the minor pentatonic scale for soloing—even if the rhythm guitar or keyboard player is playing major chords! Blues almost always uses the minor pentatonic scale. Why? First of all, the only rule worth remembering in music is this: If it sounds good to you then it works. When you apply the minor pentatonic scale to a major chord progression, you get a clash on some of the notes, and not every note will sound sweet and perfect. This clash is what gives the blues its unique style. The earliest recordings show that blues solos always used the minor pentatonic scale for improvised solos and vocal melodies. A major pentatonic scale in a blues solo would sound out of place, even though theoretically you would expect a major chord progression to have a major scale.

Rock Norms

The genre of rock music is extremely hard to define, especially because it has undergone radical changes every ten years or so. Think of the big change from the '50s sound of Elvis Presley to the '60s sound of Jimi Hendrix. The only thing that you can quantify in rock music is its connection to the blues, because that's where it came from.

Early rock and roll borrowed standard blues chord progressions as the basis for a new style. As the style evolved and grew, there was less reliance on the blues roots of early rock music. Like blues players, many rock guitarists make extensive use of the pentatonic scale for improvisation. As rock has evolved and grown into more progressive and sophisticated sounds, it has also adopted other sounds for improvisation.

Some famous pentatonic-based solos include:

- "Stairway to Heaven," by Led Zeppelin (A-minor pentatonic)
- "Purple Haze," by Jimi Hendrix (E-minor pentatonic)
- "Sweet Child of Mine," by Guns N' Roses (E-minor pentatonic)
- "Freebird," by Lynyrd Skynyrd (G-minor pentatonic)
- "Crossroads," by Eric Clapton (A-minor pentatonic)
- "Rivera Paradise," by Stevie Ray Vaughan (E-minor pentatonic)

Many guitar players use the pentatonic scale as a starting point, adding other notes to the scale to dress it up. While this may be exactly how you want to sound in the end, you have to learn to crawl before you run. Learn the basic pentatonic scale and internalize it before you move on to more advanced topics.

Voicing

While it's convenient to think of the pentatonic scales as "boxes," boxes don't make any music—notes do. So how can you think "outside the box"? Start singing everything you play. That's right, warm up those vocal chords; it's time to sing.

By singing every note you play, you create a connection between your fingers and your ears. This may be the single most important topic in this book. The thinking is simple: Every time you hear a great guitar solo, your ear learns the sound. After listening a few times, you can sing the solo in your head—this is called pitch memory. How do you get the sound from your ears to the guitar? If you haven't been playing guitar very long, playing what you hear can be difficult. You may know the scale, but your fingers may not be able to keep up with your imagination. You may have the technique, but the scales aren't yet intuitive.

The human body gives you just such an instrument for recreating sounds: your voice. Your voice can recreate almost any range of sounds you can remember. Singing the scales from the beginning, you will improve your ability to play what you hear, not just what your fingers can play. In addition, you will strengthen the connection between your hands, ears, and brain. Once your ears and hands are communicating well, you will control the sounds coming out of your instrument—rather than letting the scale shapes control you! Being able to play with that mixture of control and freedom is the goal of all improvisers.

Being Musical

No matter how many flashy licks and lines you know, being musical is more fundamental than being technical. The term "phrasing" is used to describe a player's musicality. Great phrasing is the most important element of a solo—even more important than the notes.

The evolution of pentatonic playing comes from early blues, and the sound of the blues started with singers. Singers sang pentatonic melodies, embellishing them in different ways every time they performed. Blues also grew out of the gospel music tradition where improvisatory flourishes were part of the genre—you were expected to sing something different every time. The goal for many rock and blues players has been to emulate the human voice and its improvisatory style. The great rock and blues guitar players all have one thing in common: They have a vocal-like approach to their solos.

Just listen to some great vocal music. The first thing to understand is that singers have to pause to breathe. Guitar players are notorious for playing with no break in the sound, and beginning players are especially guilty of this. Vocalists can't do this, because they must stop to breathe. Naturally, vocal solos are broken up into small phrases of three or four seconds of music.

Learn every solo you can—this is how you learn to play music. If you're unsure of where to start, the blues is a great place to begin. B.B. King's solos are a great tool for learning the blues style. Many of his solos aren't overly technical and are easy to learn. In rock music, Carlos Santana never fails to play a great solo. While he doesn't rely completely on the pentatonic scale, he uses it a great deal. These are just two examples you can use to get started.

Listen to the guitar solos of B.B. King, Albert Collins, Buddy Guy, and Clarence "Gatemouth" Brown. They all play short phrases and take musical breaths just like singers do. When you improvise, try to leave a little space every few seconds. Breaking up your solo into little parts makes the music easier for the listener to digest.

The vast majority of listeners can't appreciate the technical merits of your solos. They can't comment on how hip it was to use the B-minor pentatonic scale. All they can hear are the phrases you create. As a great teacher of mine once said, "Rests are the windows of music." Let the light shine in!

Chapter 4

Inflections and Phrasing

Inflections are the small nuances that make your signature sound unique. Slides, bends, pull-offs, hammer-ons, and vibrato are all considered inflections. When you apply inflections to notes, the result is music. If you're practicing scales and they seem cold and unmusical to you, chances are the inflections are missing.

Why It's Important

Inflection is the single most important element of playing a musical instrument. It's often overlooked and undertaught. Every musician, when given a simple melody, will approach playing it differently. Guitar is a very expressive instrument, and has many options in the inflection department, including some not found on any other instrument. All of these options define a player's signature—and touch. Inflections are a permanent part of the musical examples that appear later in this book. From now on, when I introduce a scale, you'll get a more realistic idea of how the scale actually sounds. A musical example played without inflections is akin to hearing the sound of a computer speaking. All the right information is there, but it just doesn't sound right; it's missing the inflections.

Coming Alive with Slides

Inflections are often considered ways to "dress up" a basic note. Slides are the first and simplest way to inflect a note on the guitar. They make basic melodies come alive.

To achieve a proper slide, begin by playing any fretted note on the guitar with your first finger. (You can use any finger to slide, but the first finger is easier to slide at first.) Let's start with the seventh fret on the G string—the note D. Strike the seventh fret and quickly slide your first finger up to the ninth fret E on the same string. That's a two-fret slide. If you keep the pressure of your finger down on the string while you slide, the note will continue to sound. However, if you let your finger release the pressure while you slide, you may lose the volume of the note. Keeping downward pressure is essential to a good slide. It's important to know that you pick only the first note, and you don't need to restrike the note at the end of the slide. It's like riding a bike—you pedal once and then coast on the energy you create. Pick once, and transfer the sound up one fret by sliding.

FIGURE 4-1
Two-fret slide

TRACK 8

It's a great effect. As you practice sliding, you'll become faster and more adept at keeping the correct pressure on the string. **FIGURE 4-1** shows you the slide I just described.

Slide Options

What can you do with a slide? Anything you want. You can slide from above or below any note you want. You can even slide from great distances above a note, as long as you slide on the same string! Slides are very useful for softening the attack on the second note you play. When you pick every note you play, the effect can be broken and

FIGURE 4-2 "Mary Had a Little Lamb" with slides

TRACK 9

choppy. By using a lot of slides, you pick less. Slides help achieve a smooth, polished, and professional sound.

Slides also give a slippery effect from note to note, because you are sliding through chromatic notes. Chromatic notes are the notes, or semitones, between normal scale tones. By sliding, you connect the scale tones with the other, less frequently played notes.

One important aspect of sliding that you must understand is that you need to slide into the destination note; you can't just slide aimlessly. For a good example of this, look at **FIGURE 4-2**, "Mary Had a Little Lamb."

The first line of music shows the bare example with no slides. The second line of music shows how you can dress up a simple melody with slides. Notice that the slides in this example all start below the melody notes. If the fifth fret is the melody note, start on a lower fret and slide into the fifth fret. This is what the term "destination" means; you have to know where you're sliding to. You can always slide from either one or two frets below any key melody note. Let your ear be the ultimate judge of when and how to slide.

Pentatonic with Slides

A great place to use the sliding technique is the pentatonic scale. **FIGURE 4-3** takes the basic minor pentatonic scale and adds a few slides into some of the notes played with the first finger.

FIGURE 4-3   A-minor pentatonic scale with slides from below

TRACK 10

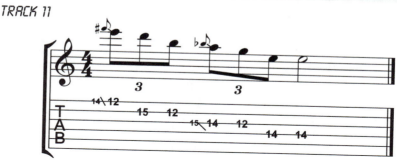

FIGURE 4-4 E-minor pentatonic scale with slides from above

TRACK 11

This simple inflection transforms the scale into something much more than just a scale—now it's music. **FIGURE 4-4** uses slides from above notes of the major pentatonic scale. Notice how this slide gives us a "bluesy" feel. Slides are pivotal to understanding blues playing.

There is no limit to what you can slide. Use your imagination and, most important, your ears to create examples of your own. As a fan, you should study your favorite players and listen to the subtle slides that are a part of their playing.

The Mechanics of a Bend

For many players, bends are the unique part of guitar playing. While it's true that other instruments are capable of bending pitch, few have the variety of bends to rival the guitar.

A bend is performed by horizontally pushing a string. While any finger can bend a note, your third and fourth fingers are best suited for the job. Bending is a strength-in-numbers exercise; one finger has a much harder time bending a note than three fingers do. On guitar, the finger that plays the highest fret is the finger that sounds. You can place your other fingers behind any note you play to prove this; no matter what you do behind a note, the highest fret will sound. When you bend, the other fingers help you bend the note up. Using multiple fingers to bend is crucial to proper bending.

It looks pretty dramatic—you push the string far away from its usual position. This is normal. At first you may be afraid of breaking the string, but don't worry; guitar strings are made to be bent.

ALERT!

To get the most use out of your guitar, a proper setup is important. Improper string height, fret problems, and intonation problems can make playing the guitar harder to play and less enjoyable. Take your guitar to a qualified service technician every six months to ensure that your guitar is in top form.

The location of the note on the guitar is also important in a bend. The closer you are to the nut of the guitar, the harder it is to bend the string. The higher up the neck you go, the easier it is.

The guitar has the unique capability to play the exact same pitch (or note) on several different strings. If you have difficulty bending a particular note, finding that note somewhere else on the neck may make it easier to bend. The type of guitar you play will also affect how well you can bend. Electric guitars with light gauge strings will be much easier to bend on than an acoustic guitar with heavier gauge strings.

Standard Half-Step Bends

The interval of a half step is the distance between adjacent frets. For example, the distance between the second and the third fret on any string is a half step. Half steps are the smallest distance between any two notes in the Western music system. When you bend a string a half step, you push the string one note sharp. A bend is just another way to change the pitch of a note. If you bend a note, the bent note may not fit with what you're playing. Just as you must slide to the destination note, you have to bend to the correct note. If you play a scale and want to include a half-step bend, you can bend only certain notes in the scale. What matters is how far away the next note is. **FIGURE 4-5** shows a simple major scale with half-step bends included.

The only notes that you can bend a half step are the notes that are followed by a half step, or the interval of one fret. If your next note is any farther away than one fret, a half-step bend won't work. Half-step bends are less common than other bends because most scales, whether pentatonic or major or minor, contain more whole steps than half steps. The most common bend is the whole-step bend.

Whole-Step Bends

Whole-step bends are the most common bends in rock and blues guitar playing. The interval of a whole step, which is twice as large as a half step, is the distance between two frets. When you bend a whole step, you push the string twice as far as you do in a half-step bend. Pentatonic

FIGURE 4-5   Major scale with half-step bends

TRACK 12

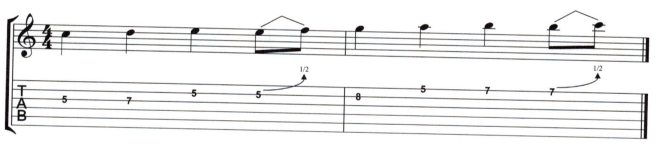

FIGURE 4-6   A-minor pentatonic scale with whole step bends

TRACK 13

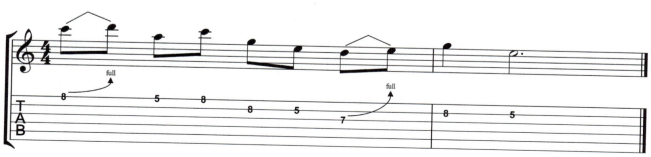

scales are rife with bending possibilities. Take any pentatonic scale (major or minor) and all the notes that you play with the third or fourth fingers can be bent a whole step. **FIGURE 4-6** is an example of an A-minor pentatonic scale with whole step bends on the third and fourth fingers.

It's important to mention that by bending, you aren't adding any new notes to the scale. The pentatonic scale hasn't been altered; the bends go from one note in the scale to the next. These bends can take a bland example and give it life. Guitarists often associate bending with emotional playing; bending can sound like a wailing cry.

Bend Kindly

Bending is a great technique when done well. When done poorly, it can yield some less than positive results. Bending involves tuning the bent note. You're essentially pushing the string out of tune and stopping on a different note that you will also have to tune. As you've noticed from tuning your guitar, a small turn of the peg can make a big difference. When you're bending, it's important to bend in tune.

Bending a string can be strenuous on the muscles in your wrist, so don't overdo your bending practice because you can strain your muscles. At the first sign of any pain or tingling in your hands, stop immediately and take a thirty-minute break. If the pain persists, see a physician immediately. Hand pain can cripple your ability to play, but with proper treatment can be healed.

Tuning a Bend

Tuning a bend takes practice. At first you may not be perfect at it, but the old adage holds up: Practice makes perfect. How can you practice playing a bend in tune? One easy way is to use a tuner. Try bending half steps and whole steps into your tuner and letting the tuner show you how close you are. A chromatic tuner is the only tuner capable of helping you tune a bend. A standard guitar tuner is taught to recognize only the sound of the open strings and will not be able to tune every bent note.

Chromatic tuners can tune and hear every note on the guitar. This makes them ideal for tuning your bends.

As you use the tuner to practice your bends, your ears will learn the sound of a perfectly bent string. Bending out of tune is like playing an out-of-tune guitar; no one wants to hear a guitarist play out of tune—it hurts!

Another way to practice bending is to determine what note you are bending to. For example, bending the twelfth fret of the third string up a whole step gives you the note A. How do you know this? The note on the twelfth fret is G. The minute you bend any note, you change the name of that note. When you bend the G up a whole step you change the note to A (your tuner will verify this). If you don't have a tuner handy, you can use the fourteenth fret as a reference pitch. Remember, whole steps are two frets away, so the bent twelfth fret will sound like the pitch of the fourteenth.

The example in **FIGURE 4-7** is a unique situation where you have a bent note on one string, and on the next string you have an unbent note of the same pitch.

Both notes are the identical E. The only difference is that each one falls on a different string. By playing them this way you're able to play both Es together. If the bent E isn't in tune, you'll hear the notes clash with one another. When both notes are in tune perfectly, they will blend together into one sound. This is called a unison bend. Jimi Hendrix was a big fan of this bend; it's all over his playing.

FIGURE 4-7   Playing two Es, one bent, one fretted normally

TRACK 14

Advanced Bends

The remaining bends are all related to half- and whole-step bends. Each has a slight variation in the attack and release. These bends are very expressive and, once again, mimic the human voice. These bends are common among great lead players and you should recognize them quickly.

Pre-Bend

The pre-bend is a simple variation that involves bending the note up before striking the note. Pre-bends can be applied to any type of half-step or whole-step bend. Check out the following example of a pre-bend in **FIGURE 4-8**.

FIGURE 4-8   Pre-bend

TRACK 15

FIGURE 4-9   C-minor pentatonic scale with full bends and pre-bends

TRACK 16

The pre-bend can be difficult to master. On other bends, your ear can tell you when to stop (when it's in tune). But on a pre-bend, you have to stretch the note up before you hear it. This means that your hands have to know exactly where to place the bend because you can't hear it until the string is played. If you've practiced bending for a while, your hands will start to feel the "sweet spot" where the notes are in tune. **FIGURE 4-9** uses pre-bends and standard bends. Notice the difference in the notation for each bend. As you get more used to reading guitar tablature and notation, you'll be able to accurately read the symbols.

Bend and Release

A bend and release is a simple variation on a common bend. You bend up, and then you release the string back to its normal position. In the following bend and release example shown in **FIGURE 4-10**, notice that the released note is in brackets; this means you don't restrike that note. It just keeps sounding.

Another simple variation of the bend and release is created by varying the speed. You may wish to bend up quickly, and release very slowly. You can do the opposite. You can do whatever you want!

FIGURE 4-10   Bend and release in a D-minor pentatonic scale

TRACK 17

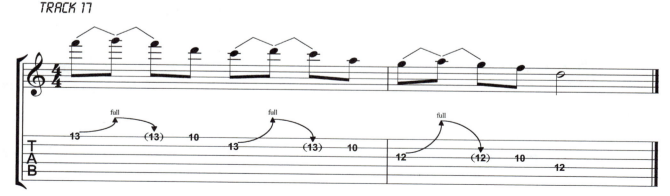

Tremolo Bends

A tremolo is a device that enables you to change the tension of the strings. Tremolos are built into the bridges of most guitars and have a piece of metal that screws into the bridge so you can rock the bridge back and forth to change the pitch as you please. Because tremolos allow you to change the tension of the strings, they bend notes in a very different way than your fingers do.

When you bend a string with your finger, you can only raise the pitch. Up to this point, all the bends you've played have gone from a low note to a higher note. But with a conventional tremolo, which is found on Stratocaster-type guitars, you can easily bend the pitch *down* by using the bar to bend the string down. All the bend types you've just learned can be done this way, even pre-bends. If you have a guitar equipped with a Floyd-Rose® tremolo, you can bend pitch up *and* down. One of the masters of the tremolo is modern rocker Steve Vai. His album *Passion and Warfare* is an encyclopedia of guitar techniques. Vai has taken the ability to bend notes with his tremolo and fingers to an art from. Other interesting tremolo players are Eddie Van Halen, Allan Holdsworth, and Stevie Ray Vaughan.

Practice using your tremolo to bend notes from any of the previous examples. Simply substitute the tremolo bar instead of your finger bends.

Non-Bending Inflections

There are other inflections you can use to create interesting sounds and to help pull your musical style together.

Hammer-ons

Hammer-ons are similar to slides. Slides let you play a second note without striking again, giving you a smoother connection between the notes. Hammer-ons also let you play a second note without striking it with the pick; but instead of sliding into the note, you hammer your finger into the string forcing it to sound. Hammer-ons go from a lower note you pick to a higher note you hammer-on. For example, play a fifth

FIGURE 4-11   Hammer-ons in the E-minor pentatonic scale

TRACK 18

fret G string with your first finger and pick that note, then with your third finger hit the seventh fret.

The term "hammer-on" isn't just a funny phrase—you really need to hammer your finger down. To make the note sound properly, you have to strike the string quite hard. **FIGURE 4-11** shows how to apply a hammer-on to a pentatonic scale in the key of E minor. Hammer-ons are great for building technique and coordination in your fret hand.

Hammering-on and pulling-off instead of relying on picking is called legato technique. The undisputed master of legato technique is British rock and jazz player Allan Holdsworth. His unique rock/jazz album *Metal Fatigue* showcases his mastery of legato style.

Pull-offs

The pull-off, unlike the hammer-on, begins on a higher note and pulls off to a lower note. In **FIGURE 4-12**, let's apply pull-offs to an E-minor pentatonic scale.

To pull-off correctly, let your third finger actually pull the string down. You can't just release your finger because the note would not sound. Imagine that the tip of your finger is like a pick, and you have to pull the fingertip through the string to make a sound. It should create a slight snap. The snap acts like a pick and sets the string in motion. **FIGURE 4-13** combines pull-offs and hammer-ons using an A-minor pentatonic scale. The hammer-ons are used as the scale ascends, and the pull-offs while the scale descends.

FIGURE 4-12 Pull-offs in the E-minor pentatonic scale

TRACK 19

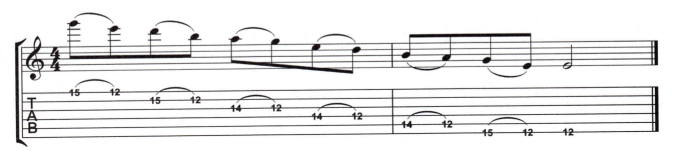

FIGURE 4-13 Hammer-ons and pull-offs in the A-minor pentatonic scale

TRACK 20

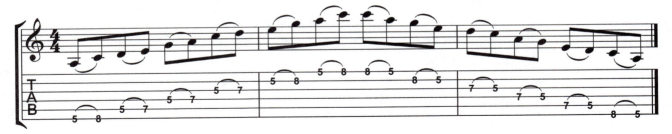

Acoustic guitars are harder to hammer-on and pull-off due to their larger string gauges. Electric guitars use smaller strings and are easier to hammer-on and pull-off.

Vibrato

Vibrato is a slight fluctuation in pitch that helps long notes sound fuller and less stagnant. This effect can be performed on almost every instrument imaginable, with the notable exception of piano and clarinet. On guitar, vibrato is an extremely common way to dress up long notes, and is achieved by rapidly pushing the string up and down. Most people

FIGURE 4-14 A long note held with and without vibrato

TRACK 21

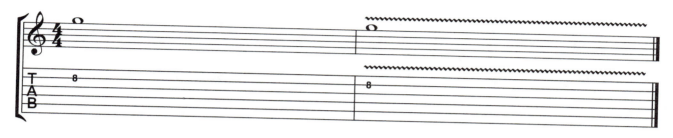

will agree that notes with vibrato sound and sustain better. **FIGURE 4-14** shows a long note at first without vibrato, and then with vibrato.

Each player has his or her own unique vibrato style. Vibrato can be very slow, or it can be very fast. Technically, vibrato is done from a shake of the wrist. The fingers help control the speed of the vibrato, but the wrist provides the energy. Listen to your favorite players and see what kind of vibrato they use. B.B. King is famous for his short and quick "bee-sting" vibrato. David Gilmour of Pink Floyd uses a slower and wider vibrato. Check out the solo on "Shine On You Crazy Diamond" for a great example of his slow vibrato. Ⓔ

Chapter 5

Beyond the Pentatonic Scale

The pentatonic scale—though learning it is a crucial first step—can be limiting musically. Many players feel confined by the "box" shape and wish to "break out" of the box. There are some simple things you can do to go beyond the basic scale. This chapter expands your knowledge and gets you playing great music without getting too complicated.

FIGURE 5-1 A-minor pentatonic scale, fingerboard diagram

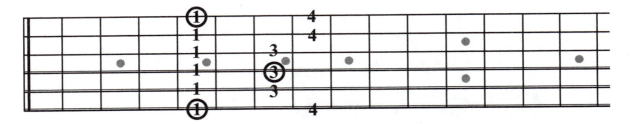

More Than Meets the Eye

FIGURE 5-2 Full fingerboard diagram

So far, the pentatonic scales you've played have started on the low E string and have a familiar box pattern to them. Both the major and the minor pentatonic scales are based out of the same box pattern. You may start to feel confined in this scale—there must be something more, you say to yourself. You're in luck! With a little bit of brainpower, you can take the pentatonic concept and expand upon it.

Let's take a look at FIGURE 5-1 and at the notes that make up an A-minor pentatonic scale: A, C, D, E, and G. (Remember "penta" means five notes.)

You'll notice that there are two circled notes in this scale. That's because scales contain repeated notes.

Do you think that the fifth fret pentatonic shape in FIGURE 5-1 is the only way to play this scale? Think again. It's not! If you think of the scales as notes and not as a shape, you can figure out other ways to play this scale across the neck. Let's look at the entire neck and every note that's found on it. FIGURE 5-2 shows every pitch on every fret.

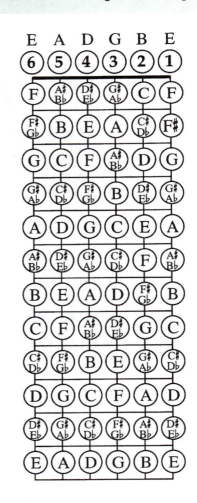

FIGURE 5-3   A-minor pentatonic scale throughout the entire fingerboard

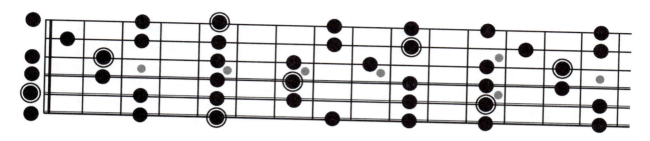

Can you find A, C, D, E, F, and G in other places? **FIGURE 5-3** shows the notes from the A-minor pentatonic scale (A, C, D, E, G) in spots all over the neck.

See how the notes repeat all across the fingerboard? These are all the possible ways to play the A-minor pentatonic scale. From these notes you can extract five moveable positions of the pentatonic scale. If you know the scales all over the neck, you'll be able to play your pentatonic ideas no matter where you are.

Five Shapes of Pentatonic

There are five shapes of the pentatonic scale on the guitar neck. No matter where you start them, they always repeat in the same fashion, with the same shapes and fingerings. This is yet another way that the guitar makes life convenient for learning: repeating patterns. For our purposes, let's look at the F-minor pentatonic scale. The first position of the scale that begins on the first fret F of the sixth string will always be considered "form I." Most guitar players who play pentatonic solos start there and venture up or down the neck to the other positions.

Form I

Form I is the simplest form to remember: It's the original pentatonic scale you learned. To recap, all you have to do to play a form-I pentatonic scale is to determine two things—what the root of the scale is and whether it's major or minor. Once you know that, you can place it accordingly with the rules you learned in Chapter 3. Remember that form I of F minor is the same as form I of A flat Major since those pentatonic scales share the same notes. **FIGURE 5-4** shows form I of the F-minor pentatonic scale.

Form II

Form II continues where form I left off and continues up the fingerboard. You need to know how to find this scale as a separate entity, not something that is tied into form I. **FIGURE 5-5** shows the form-II pentatonic scale in the key of F minor.

When multiple notes are circled, the root has been repeated elsewhere in the scale. To place this scale you need to locate where the

FIGURE 5-4   F-minor pentatonic scale form I

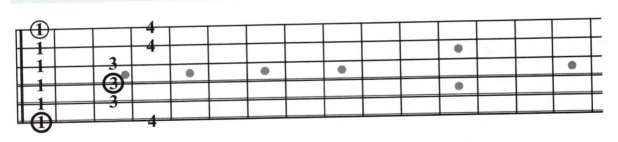

FIGURE 5-5   F-minor pentatonic scale form II

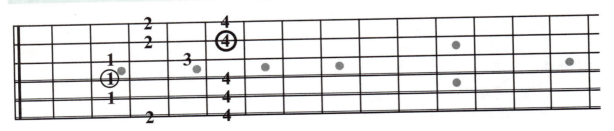

root is. Form II is tricky because the lowest note is not the root; you have to look inside the middle of the scale to find the root. Once you've found the root, you can move this shape to any other key just as you did with the earlier forms. The two circled notes indicate that the scale contains a repeated note. The note F, which is the root, comes back in other parts of the scale. All five forms of the pentatonic scale are completely moveable into every key—just move the root. For the F-minor scale, the root is found on the third string, third fret F. Follow the fingerboard chart in **FIGURE 5-2** to help you find the roots at first. As you play more and apply these new scales, you'll start to remember the notes on the fingerboard. If you play in the same keys, you will learn those notes easily. Practice makes perfect!

Form III

FIGURE 5-6's neck diagram shows the overall shape of form III. The root of this scale is on the fifth string, on the eighth fret F.

Just as you can do with the scales you learned in previous chapters, you can move these scales to any key as long as you place the root on the correct note. You don't always have to start on the root, but it may help at first to start there. As you get more comfortable with the shapes, you'll use the root as a guide and start anywhere in the shape you feel like starting. Remember, notes are just options; explore the ones you want!

FIGURE 5-6 F-minor pentatonic form III

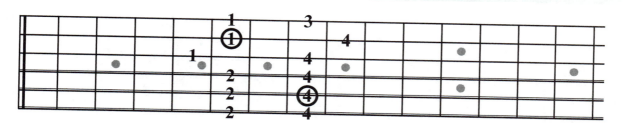

Form IV

Form IV is an easier shape to deal with because it greatly resembles form I. The root of this scale is on the fifth string, eighth fret. This is the same root as form III, but unlike form III, this scale starts with your first finger and yields a totally different shape. **FIGURE 5-7** is a neck diagram of this scale.

Form IV is simpler because its root is on the fifth string. Anyone who has played a lot of moveable chord shapes on the low sixth and fifth strings knows the names of those notes, making this scale easy to place since you can recognize F quickly and start the F scale there, for example. Visually, form IV shares a shape similar to form I, just altering one fret on the second string. Form IV is a nice in-between point for your scale playing. If your form I scale is low on the neck as F is, form IV is halfway up the neck and will allow you to hear the same notes higher on the neck.

Form IV of the pentatonic is the most useful scale to master because it puts you in a very different part of the neck than form I does.

FIGURE 5-7   F-minor pentatonic form IV

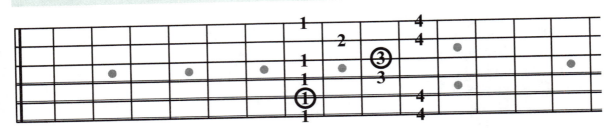

FIGURE 5-8   F-minor pentatonic form V

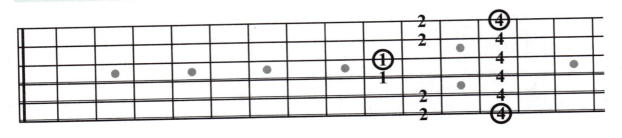

Form V

Form V is the final pentatonic scale position, and its root is found on the sixth string. Wait—doesn't form I have its root on the sixth string? Yes it does! What makes form V different is that your fourth finger plays the root in this shape, not your first finger as in form I. **FIGURE 5-8** is a neck diagram of the final shape, form V.

As a general rule, if you start from different fingers on the same note, the shape will change completely. In the end, you don't have to master every note on the neck to play these shapes. This chart will help you learn where these shapes are placed:

Form	Starting Finger	String
I	First finger	Sixth string
II	First finger	Fourth string
III	Fourth finger	Fifth string
IV	First finger	Fifth string
V	Fourth finger	Sixth string

As you can see from the chart, to be able to place these scales effectively, you need to know the roots on only the sixth, fifth, and fourth strings.

Shape Conclusions

As you might have guessed, you haven't gone beyond the pentatonic scale. What you've really done is explored the entire neck with it. To really go beyond the shapes, you have to view the entire neck as a whole and use bits from each shape freely. As you progress, your ability to move from one shape to another will grow.

Ideally, you should know all the notes that are available to you. In the end, you can pick and choose the notes you want. **FIGURE 5-9** shows an F-minor pentatonic scale that uses every position in one long example.

Notice how the scales are connected with slides that help join the positions. What you get in the end is a very long scale. This example

FIGURE 5-9 F-minor pentatonic scale using all positions

TRACK 22

isn't playable in just one shape; you must use all the shapes to get through this. Pentatonic boxes can be easy to spot when you watch another player solo; the player doesn't have to move his or her hand at all. When you play this kind of example, people who don't play guitar won't know what you're doing! You'll use the entire neck in one lick. You paid for the whole neck, might as well explore it.

Adding to the Scale

Some of music's greatest moments have been total mistakes. Mistakes in fingerings of chords can lead to interesting and unusual chord shapes. While you were practicing the pentatonic scale, maybe you hit a wrong note—a note that was outside of the scale shape you were supposed to play. What if that note didn't sound bad at all? What if you really liked that note? Some disciplined students would just correct the mistake and move on to the "real" scale. Others would morph the original scale and add the "happy accident" to the scale and create an entirely new scale.

The Blues Scale

The blues scale is a minor pentatonic scale with an added note. It's not really considered a six-note scale because the added note is considered a passing tone; you use it to get from one note in the scale to the next note smoothly. The added note has gained acceptance over the years, and the five notes with the passing tone have grown into their own scale—the blues scale.

FIGURE 5-10 is an example of an A-minor blues scale.

Notice how the shape is the same as the minor pentatonic scale; you just add the note E♭ to the scale. The E♭ helps smooth out the jump between the D and the E normally found in the minor pentatonic scale. The passing tone of E♭ has long been used by singers and is another way that vocalists have influenced instrumental soloists. You can use the blues scale in place of a normal minor pentatonic scale—they substitute for each other. The added E♭ is a very bluesy note and will add spice to your original scale. You don't have to play the blues to use the scale; many rock players find it effective in rock solos.

Hexatonic

"Hexa" means "six," so it stands to reason that a hexatonic scale is a six-note scale. Many players find that by adding one note to the pentatonic scale, they can yield some incredibly fresh sounds. Let's go back to the original A-minor pentatonic scale that contains the notes A, C, D, E,

FIGURE 5-10   A-minor blues scale

TRACK 23

FIGURE 5-11   A-minor hexatonic scale

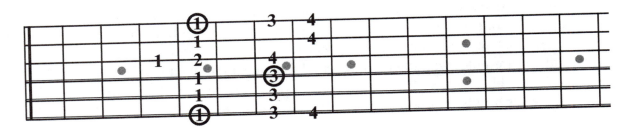

and G. To make this pentatonic scale into a hexatonic scale, you add the note B. **FIGURE 5-11** is the new hexatonic scale in A.

Adding one note changes a lot doesn't it?

Now for a Little Theory

We added the note B. While that's the "name" of the tone, knowing the name of the note only helps us in one key. For instance, what note do you add to an F-minor pentatonic scale to make it hexatonic? You could move the A-minor example to F and figure it out, but that's taking the long way home. Music theory uses numbers to designate the distance between notes. The term for this distance is an interval. The interval from A to B is simply a second. (There's more on this in Chapter 7.)

We call it a second because the distance from A to B is two; B is the second note of an A scale. Seconds are also always two frets above any note. Just as A is the fifth fret, B is the seventh fret. No matter where you are on the guitar, seconds are always two frets above the root. So what I'm really saying is that the hexatonic scale is a minor pentatonic scale with an added second. If we call it a second, it can apply to any key and any scale.

Second Helping

The hexatonic scale sounds slightly more melodic than the pentatonic scale. The addition of the second interval helps smooth the distances between the notes. Most melodies that are sung contain small intervals between the notes. Melodies that are termed "lyrical" are based on close intervals. The pentatonic scale has some large jumps between the notes that can make it hard to be lyrical. When you play the hexatonic scale, the added note helps smooth out the scale and makes it more melodic. To hear a master of the pentatonic and hexatonic scales, listen to Eric Johnson's "Cliffs of Dover."

If you don't have total command of the fingerboard, adding the second interval to the F-minor pentatonic is easier said than done. You may want to go back to your charts and add the note. Since the five forms of pentatonic are in the key of F, you should try to make those forms into hexatonic scales. The interval of a second when applied to F is the note G. Just add two frets to the root to find the second. Go back through every form and add that note to each shape. Use the fingerboard chart in **FIGURE 5-2** to help you find all the Gs.

You'll discover that certain forms work better for hexatonic than others. If you'd like to adapt your own scales, you'll find that neck paper is the single most helpful tool for working scales out. Being able to see the entire neck is crucial to playing the scale fully. If you stumble upon a "happy accident" note, try to work it out all over the neck. Neck paper is available at most music stores. In a pinch, get a ruler and draw your own.

Another Hexatonic Scale

The term "hexatonic" defines the scale as containing six notes. It doesn't specifically tell you what the extra note is. Another variation on the hexatonic scale involves adding the sixth (instead of the second). Sixths, while they might sound far away, are actually not hard to find. The interval of a sixth is always three frets below the root. For example, if your root is A (fifth fret, sixth string) drop down three frets to second fret F♯ and you have the sixth. This technique is great for finding the name of the sixth tone. Now that you know the name of the note, you have to place it inside the pentatonic scales. In a form-I A-minor pentatonic scale, you won't add the second fret F♯—that would be a real stretch. Instead, consult your fingerboard chart to find the F♯ that fell more comfortably under your fingers. **FIGURE 5-12** shows a form-I A-minor pentatonic scale with an added sixth.

The sixth is a wonderful-sounding note; it blends right into the scale and provides nice color to the scale. Applying this hexatonic scale to the blues gives you a very tasty result. Check out **FIGURE 5-13**, an A-minor hexatonic scale with a sixth added. The example contains bends and slides discussed in the last chapter. Notice how all the small elements fit together to make a great result. The more you study the small parts of playing guitar, the greater impact it will have on your overall playing.

FIGURE 5-12   A hexatonic scale (adding a sixth to a minor pentatonic)

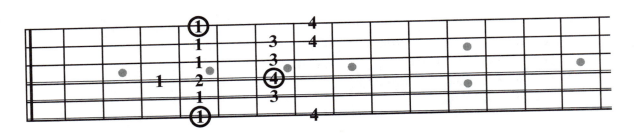

   FIGURE 5-13   A-minor hexatonic blues lick

TRACK 24

FIGURE 5-14   Septatonic scale

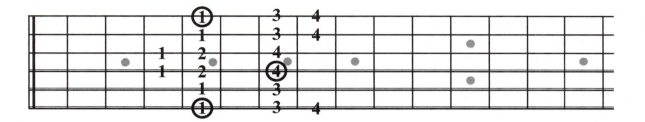

The Septatonic Scale

You looked at two different examples of the hexatonic scale: one with a second, and one with a sixth. What about combining the second and the sixth notes into the pentatonic, forming a seven-note pentatonic scale? We could call it a septatonic scale. Let's try it. (See **FIGURE 5-14**.)

The scale sounds good as a whole because the two notes interact well with the scale. If you like the sound of this scale, feel free to use it where you feel it's most effective. However, the truth is, there is no such thing as a septatonic scale. What you actually created by accident is a traditional scale or mode. With the exception of pentatonic and hexatonic, all scales in the Western music system are seven notes. The septatonic scale is really the Dorian scale, which is a derivative of the major scale, commonly referred to as a mode. If you enjoy the sound and possibilities of seven-note scales, you'll really enjoy learning about major and minor scales and modes in the upcoming chapters.

Building from a common ground is an effective way to learn new things. From the basic minor pentatonic you were able to add notes to make a new scale. Since all traditional scales are seven notes, and all pentatonic scales are five notes, you will have to add only two notes to any pentatonic scale to play traditional major and minor scales. (E)

Chapter 6

Major and Minor Scales

Major and minor scales form the basic building blocks of Western music. From cartoons to film scores, the sounds of major and minor scales serve as a melodic vocabulary that has been ingrained into your musical experiences from an early age. In future chapters we'll see exactly what this scale is capable of, but for now let's use the major scale as a tool to construct melodies and leads.

A Major Shift

Think of the major scale as being like DNA, the building block that makes life; in this case music. In future chapters we will see exactly what this scale is capable of; for now let's use it as a tool to construct melodies and leads.

Major scales are familiar to everyone, even though you may not know the name for it. **FIGURE 6-1** shows you how to play a simple C-Major scale in the open position.

Sounds very familiar, right? What differentiates the major scale from the pentatonic is the number of notes present in the scale. Instead of five notes, the major scale has seven. For example a C-Major scale consists of the notes C, D, E, F, G, A, B, and C; the first note (C) is the root of the scale. Every major scale always uses seven notes and always repeats the first note. Major scales use every note of the musical alphabet, and always follow the same order. Major scales have a smoother sound than pentatonic scales because they don't skip any notes.

Move Friendly

One of the great things you've probably noticed about the guitar is its ability to let you move shapes around the guitar neck with ease. In the earlier chapters, you learned to move pentatonic scales, barre chords, and power chords. Major and minor scales aren't left out of the fun; they can be moved just as easily. However, what you see in **FIGURE 6-1** is *not* moveable. How can you tell? Any shape that contains open strings is not

FIGURE 6-1   C-Major scale in open position

TRACK 25

perfectly moveable. For a shape to move you must be playing all fretted notes, or "closed positions." **FIGURE 6-2** shows a simple C-Major scale that is moveable.

This shape can be played in any key—just move the first note and keep the finger pattern the same. Just like chords, scales can be thought of as little pictures. While they aren't as easy to visualize as the pentatonic scale is, the shape isn't too complex. Make sure to memorize the shape, because it's going to come in really handy.

Beyond Simple Major

In Chapter 5, you were able to generate five shapes for the pentatonic scale by mapping out the notes all across the neck. The same technique can be applied to major scales. Let's stay in C Major for now and use the notes of the C-Major scale: C, D, E, F, G, A, B, C. This is an easy scale to memorize because it doesn't use any sharps or flats.

FIGURE 6-3 maps out all the notes of C Major all over the neck.

FIGURE 6-2   Moveable C-Major scale

FIGURE 6-3   C Major across the whole neck

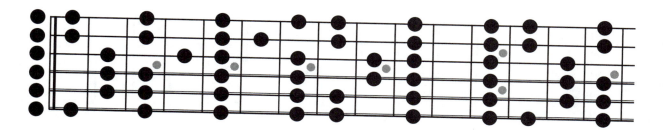

The scale diagram looks huge and very intimidating, but don't worry. We can simplify it greatly and extract positions and shapes to make it simple. A full neck diagram shows all the notes you can use, but you don't have to use all of them right from the get-go. A good analogy is the dictionary. The dictionary contains just about every word you could ever use in the English language, but you don't have to use them all. You use whatever vocabulary is comfortable and efficient. As you grow older you learn more and more effective words—as you mature as a guitar player, you will use more of the notes in this neck diagram. At first it may seem daunting, but you can break it down into simple moveable shapes.

Root Thinking

The easiest way to learn to play a scale is from the root. The root of a scale is the same as any other root you've encountered so far; it's the lowest note and it names the chord or scale you're using. In the following examples C is used as the root of the major scales. For every root on the guitar, there is a scale shape that you can play from that note. Every string contains one root; that's the beauty of a guitar string. Every note in the musical alphabet is found at least once on every string. **FIGURE 6-4** shows the locations of every C on the guitar—there are six, one for each string.

From these Cs you can place major scale shapes. In theory, there should be six positions of the major scale to play. But for a scale to be

FIGURE 6-4   Cs on the fret board

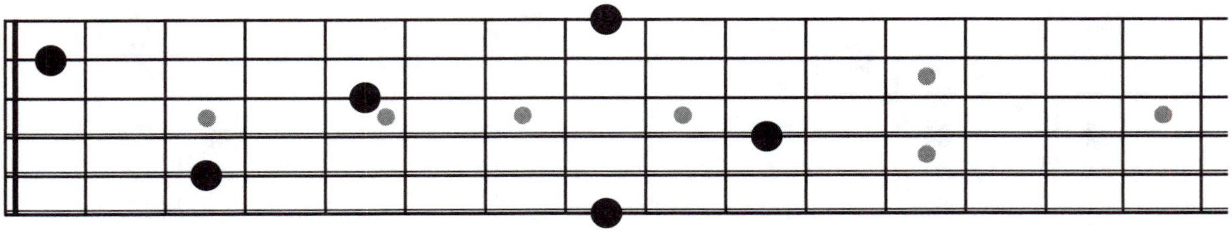

effective and moveable, you need efficient fingering. Scales that shift all over the neck have their use, but learning simpler shapes first is better. The six Cs aren't good candidates for starting a scale. For our purposes, the scale will take three strings to complete, so starting on the second or first string won't work, because you'll run out of room. You can start these scales from the sixth, fifth, fourth, and third strings, so there are four shapes to learn. Each of these shapes is completely moveable.

Moveable Scale Shapes

Break down the following simple scale shapes string by string. For any of theses scales, don't just play them in C; move them around and practice changing keys. Knowing a scale only in C helps you only if your song is in C! Try applying different scales to songs you can play right away.

Major Scale Root on the Sixth String

FIGURE 6-5 shows a simple one-octave major scale with the root on the second finger on the low E string. It's called one octave because the scale goes up only until it hits the root of C and then turns around and goes down again.

Try playing all of your scale examples in E, A, D, and G Major. These are very typical guitar keys to play in. The better you know these keys, the more prepared you will be for anything you want to create.

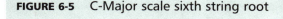

FIGURE 6-5 C-Major scale sixth string root

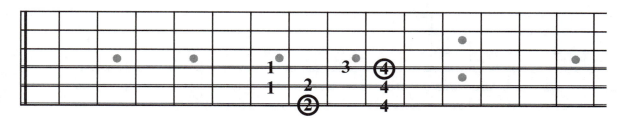

Major Scale Root on the Fifth String

Talk about convenient: The shape you just learned for the sixth string is the same shape when you start on the fifth string! **FIGURE 6-6** shows the C-Major scale with the root on the fifth string.

While the finger pattern is the same between the sixth string and the fifth string, you still have to know where C is on both strings to place it correctly. Again, memorizing the note names on the low strings will make this much easier.

FIGURE 6-6   C-Major scale fifth string root

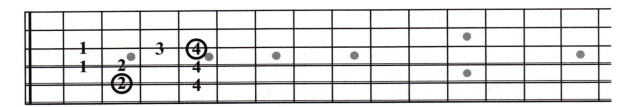

FIGURE 6-7   C-Major scale fourth string root

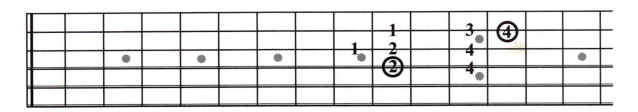

FIGURE 6-8   C-Major scale third string root

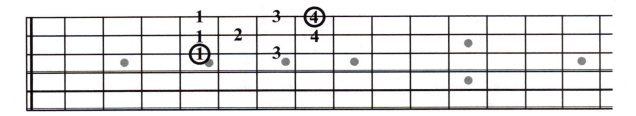

Major Scale Root on the Fourth String

When you start on the fourth string, the shape changes. **FIGURE 6-7** shows the new scale shape on the fourth string.

Major Scale Root on the Third String

This is the last string that you place scales on. While it's possible to place a scale on a higher string—for example, the second or first—the amount of shifting required would make the scale awkward and clumsy. **FIGURE 6-8** shows the C-Major scale on the third string.

This scale starts with the first finger, unlike the previous scales that all began with the second finger. This scale shape is very comfortable to play; the shape falls into your hand well.

Making Music with the Major Scale

Now that you've loaded your hands up with lots of shapes, let's try to apply these scale shapes to music. Without actually applying what you know, this is just useless info. So where do you use the major scales? Simply put, if you can use the major pentatonic scale in a song, you can use the major scale in its place, because the two scales substitute for each other. They substitute so well because they contain the same notes; the pentatonic scale just leaves out a few notes from the major. Look at the notes of a C-Major scale and a C-Major pentatonic scale, and compare:

C-Major scale: C, D, E, F, G, A, B, C
C-Major pentatonic scale: C, D, E, G, A, C

As you can see from the two scales, the major scale contains two extra notes: F and B. These notes round out the major scale and give it a more complete sound. The major pentatonic scale is actually a modified form of the major scale that purposely leaves those notes out. In short, since both scales come from the same place, you can use either scale.

Let your ears be the ultimate guide as to what you should use. **FIGURE 6-9** shows a nice major scale example over an E-Major chord.

When you study an example, pay attention to several things. First, notice that the example doesn't just play up and down the scale; that isn't musical. You have to "juggle" the notes of the scale around to be musical. Look at the next example in **FIGURE 6-10** of an interesting way to juggle notes around.

If you remember from the full-scale diagram of **FIGURE 6-3**, there are a lot of ways to play this scale. The four scale shapes I discussed just scratch the surface, but they do provide the best place to start. If you can fully memorize those four shapes all over the neck, and improvise with them, you're on your way. These scales serve as options. The more options you have when you go to play the guitar, the more creative you can be.

FIGURE 6-9 E-Major scale example

TRACK 26

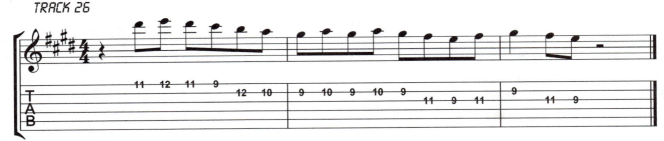

FIGURE 6-10 E-Major scale with notes juggled

TRACK 27

The Minor Scale

The minor scale is the next scale you should really have control of. Minor scales contain seven notes, just like major scales. The moveable positions are the most useful ways to play the minor scale. The following examples are in E minor, which is a key you'll play a lot of rock and blues in, so it's a logical scale to start with.

Remember, your ability to move these scales into different keys is the most important goal. Learning scales in just one key will restrict you to playing in only that one key. Many musicians explain the difference between major and minor as a difference in feeling. Major has a happy feeling, and minor has a sad feeling. While this may sound silly, many film and TV music composers use minor sounds during sad scenes, and major sounds during joyous ones.

Minor Scale Sixth String Root

Just like the major scale, the minor scale is a completely moveable scale position. Since this scale form starts with the first finger, just shift the scale to whatever key you want. **FIGURE 6-11** shows an E-minor scale with a sixth string root.

Minor Scale Fifth String Root

The major scale position is the same whether you start it on the sixth string or the fifth string, making it easy to remember. Same goes for the minor scale; the pattern is the same on the fifth string as it is on the sixth string. Look at **FIGURE 6-12**.

FIGURE 6-11   E-minor scale sixth string root

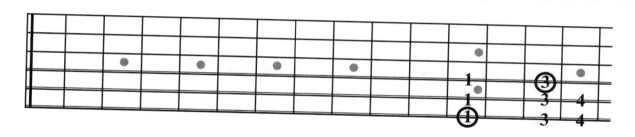

FIGURE 6-12   E-minor scale fifth string root

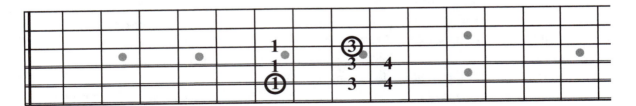

FIGURE 6-13   Locations of both Es on sixth and fifth strings

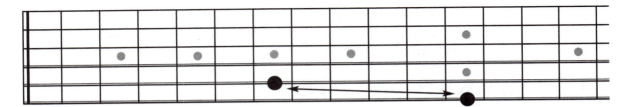

Remember that while the shape stays the same, the locations of the notes on the sixth and fifth strings are different. When you play an E-minor scale on the fifth string, it has the same shape as the sixth string form, but you have to move it to a different fret to stay in the same key. You can't just move it up one string and ignore the placement of the root. Look at **FIGURE 6-13** and note how the root moves from the twelfth fret of the sixth string, to the seventh fret of the fifth string.

Minor Scale Fourth- and Third-String Roots

Since you know the drill by now, here are the last two scale forms of minor, starting on the fourth and third strings. Look at **FIGURES 6-14** and **6-15** to learn these shapes, too, so you can play the minor scales comfortably all over the neck.

Putting the Minor Scale to Use

Where do you use the minor scales? Just as the major scale is a substitute for the major pentatonic, the minor scale is a substitute for the

FIGURE 6-14   E-minor scale fourth string root

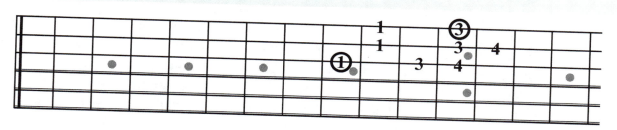

FIGURE 6-15   E-minor scale third string root

FIGURE 6-16   E-minor scale lick

TRACK 28

minor pentatonic. The minor scale and the minor pentatonic scale share notes, too. In rock music, a large number of rock songs are in minor keys. The heavier the music gets, the more minor it seems to be, making the minor scale a must-know. Experiment with the minor scales in place of pentatonics in your favorite songs. **FIGURE 6-16** shows an E-minor lick you can try.

Performance-Ready Scales

So far, all of the major and minor scales you've learned have been small seven-note scales. As you remember from the full fingerboard chart of C Major in **FIGURE 6-3**, there are a lot more note options than the four small positions you know. The reason for learning the small shapes is to give you an idea of how you can transfer the shape across the guitar. Sometimes these small one-octave shapes can be limiting if you want to play longer examples, but have no fear—there are much longer scale shapes that let you play without shifting around too much.

These other shapes are great for playing longer and more complicated licks. Some of the shapes are longer extensions of the small shapes, and some are new fingerings. But remember one thing: Guitarists can get very caught up in the visual component of playing guitar. If the shape changes suddenly, many players believe that the scale has also changed. While the visual component is important, it's equally important to know what notes you're playing, not just how they look in a shape pattern. If you're curious about a scale shape that you have stumbled upon, figure out what the notes are. You may find that the new scale shape plays exactly the same notes. In short, there are a great many ways to play scales and chords on guitar; what holds them together are the notes contained within the scales.

Two-Octave Major and Minor

Just by extending the scale into the second octave you can make the scales much more effective. By extending these scales upward into the second octave, you aren't adding any new notes to the scale; all you're doing is repeating the note order higher up on the neck. Both the major and minor scale shapes start with a familiar position and then add on a higher part. Again, you are building on what you already know.

FIGURE 6-17 shows a two-octave C-Major scale starting on the sixth string and extending all the way up to the first string.

It's amazing what a difference adding the second octave makes. You can take the same idea and extend the minor scale into two octaves. Look at **FIGURE 6-18**, a two-octave minor scale from the sixth string.

FIGURE 6-17   C-Major scale in two–octaves, root on the sixth string

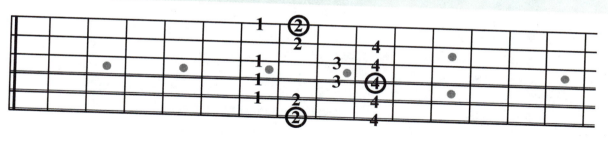

FIGURE 6-18   C-minor scale in two octaves, root on sixth string

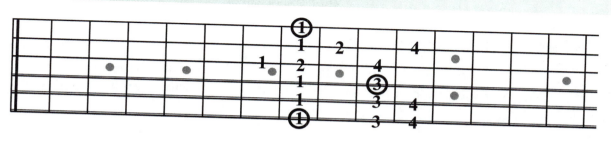

Learning longer shapes with roots on the sixth and fifth strings is an important step to being able to utilize the neck. Let's look at longer major and minor scales with roots on the fifth string. When you place a scale on the fifth string, it's harder to get the full second octave; you have only five strings to work with. To complete the second octave you have to make a shift or a slide at the top of the scale to complete the octave.

The major scale starts out with the same familiar shape and shifts up to complete the second octave This scale actually combines two smaller major scales, and you add the shift to combine them. The scales you combine are a major on the fifth string, and major on the third string. **FIGURE 6-19** shows you those scales combined into one long example.

The minor scale has a less complicated shape and stays in one spot. The only modification you make is reaching up for the last note with your pinky. This is a great minor scale shape and is very comfortable to play. Look at **FIGURE 6-20** to see this scale in action.

Three-Note-per-String Major Scales

Playing scales with three notes on every string can be very efficient. By placing three notes on every string, you end up with long runs that don't shift too far. **FIGURE 6-21** is an example of a three-note-per-string G-Major scale.

As you can see from the music, this scale covers a lot of ground. Technically, you have to stretch your fingers on the low strings, but this can be done easily. This is a great scale shape for long runs. Try playing the music in **FIGURE 6-22**, where you use hammers-ons in the scale shape.

The hammer-ons make the picking less frequent, and you can play this one really fast; it's a great showstopper lick!

Generate Materials

By now you have a good handle on the most common shapes and forms of major and minor. While this isn't all of them, these are the ones

FIGURE 6-19   C-Major scale in two octaves, root on the fifth string

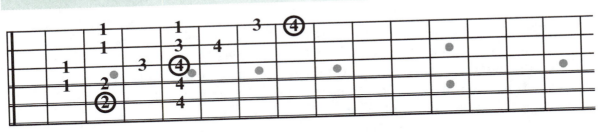

FIGURE 6-20   C-minor scale in two octaves, root on the fifth string

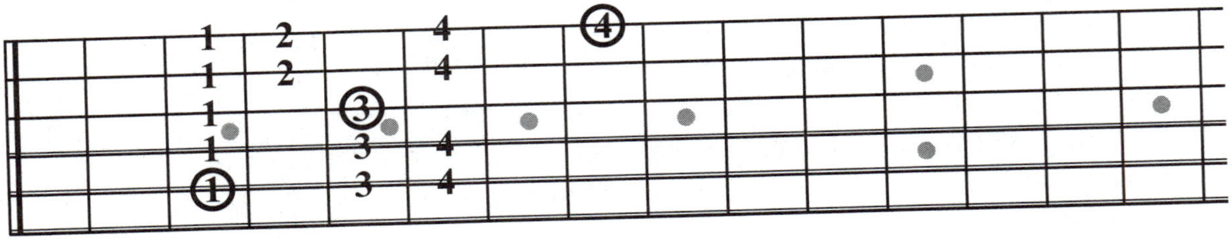

FIGURE 6-21   G-Major scale, three notes per string

TRACK 29

FIGURE 6-22   G-Major scale with hammer-ons

TRACK 30

that you need to master first. If you master these quickly, or already know a lot of these, pay great attention to the full neck diagram shown in **FIGURE 6.3**. Neck diagrams let you view the entire array of choices, and from that you can make your own scale positions if you wish. Making the diagrams is very easy—there are even computer programs to do it for you (see Chapter 19 for more on this). You now possess enough information to keep yourself busy for several lifetimes. Learning scales is a big topic, so take your time. Ⓔ

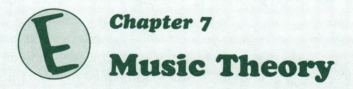

Chapter 7

Music Theory

Music theory is language that explains how music is created and constructed. Music theory helps in composing and understanding scales, and further explains how music is put together. It helps you understand why certain scales or chords sound better than others to your ears.

An Introduction to Theory

First came music; then came music theory. Music theory is merely a way to explain in an understandable way what came before it. Music theory has many practical applications because it deals with explaining sonic events in literary terms. When you hear a piece of music, trying to explain what you've heard in words can be trite and ineffective. Calling a Hendrix solo "powerful" or "moving" doesn't explain the music at all; all it does is convey an emotion that you felt while listening. While it may be more convenient to describe a piece of music as a magical moment of inspiration, the reality is that there is always something to extract from the music in terms of theory and something you can learn from it.

When you have a concrete name for something you've heard, you have the key to repeating it whenever you want. It's akin to stumbling upon a great restaurant by accident, and not asking for directions back. If you'd like to eat there again, you should ask for directions. If you hear a great chord change, or a melody that sounds unusual, to let it fly by you seems silly if you would like to integrate it into your own music. If you could figure out what you were hearing, then you would be able to recreate it in your own music.

The System

Music is based on a system that has been repeating and slowly evolving since music began. The system that holds music together is based on the interval. An interval is a measure of distance between notes—a measuring stick for musical distance. When melodies are played, the distances between the notes are intervals. When you play intervals in specific orders, you can build scales. When intervals combine and are played simultaneously, you get chords.

ESSENTIAL

The focus of this chapter is on intervals. Once you understand intervals, you'll be ready for the other music theory that is integrated throughout the rest of this book.

Straight-Line Theory

The guitar can be a wonderful instrument to study theory on, but it can also be a nightmare! It all depends how you look at the instrument. Music theory is best presented in a straight line, with everything happening consecutively one step after the other. On the guitar, to see music in a straight line, you must play across one string, meaning that you stay on one string for an exercise and you don't move, or shift, strings. You do this only to learn theory, because trying to play this way can be laborious and difficult. Being able to see the intervals based on fret distance will let you see and hear the relationships in ways that scale shapes don't let you see.

Intervals Big and Small

First is the half step, the smallest interval in the Western music system. A half step is the distance between frets—say from the first fret to the second, or from the eighth to the ninth. Whenever you move one fret, you make a half step.

The music of India utilizes microtones that are even smaller than half steps. Twentieth-century classical Western music has also experimented with microtones. On the guitar a microtone is made possible by changing the placements of the frets, or bending less than a half step.

The next interval is the whole step. The whole step is the distance between any two frets, for example the first fret to the third, or the fifth fret to the seventh. Play through the scales you've already learned, and notice where you can see whole steps and half steps easily.

There are five terms to describe the types of interval you encounter in music.

Type of Interval	Example of Interval
Major	Major second
Minor	Minor third
Perfect	Perfect fourth
Augmented	Augmented sixth
Diminished	Diminished fifth

Out of these five, the most prevalent intervals are major, minor, and perfect. Augmented and diminished, while they do occur in music, are less common than major, minor, and perfect. The names of intervals come, with a few exceptions, from the major and minor scales. If the interval is found in a major scale, it's called a major interval; if it's found in a minor scale, it's typically called a minor interval. If the interval occurs in both scales (because scales do share notes), it's called a perfect interval, because it doesn't change between the two scales. There are some exceptions to the rules that you'll learn later.

Chromatics, Flats, and Sharps

Music uses a system that contains eleven discrete notes that repeat in endless variation to form music. The eleven notes are referred to as chromatic notes. Chromatic means "every," and the chromatic scale includes every note present in music. Remember how the major and minor scales contain seven notes? The chromatic scale fills in the missing notes. **FIGURE 7-1** shows a simple chromatic scale played on the sixth string.

FIGURE 7-1 Chromatic scale played on the sixth string

Notice that this scale uses every fret in order, from 1 through 12. Every chromatic scale does this, because chromatic scales use all the notes. The musical alphabet uses seven letters: A, B, C, D, E, F, and G. But there are notes between some of these as well. The notes in between are called flats and sharps, or "accidentals." A flat lowers a pitch by one half step; a sharp raises a pitch one half step.

On a piano, the notes A, B, C, D, E, F, and G are found on the white keys. The sharps and flats are found on the raised black keys. It's easy to see the relationship between notes on a piano because of this color-coding. Every eleven notes, the pattern of white and black keys repeats itself.

Finding sharps and flats on a guitar is almost as simple: To make a note sharp, find the note's original location and raise it up one fret. For example, on the sixth string, the first fret is F. If you want an F♯, you just raise the original note by one fret, which in this case is second fret F♯. To make a flat, you lower the original note one fret. For example, on the sixth string, the third fret is G. To make it flat, subtract one fret to make it second fret G♭. But wait. You just figured out that second fret was F♯, so how can it also be G♭ on the same string? Don't fret!

Enharmonic Notes

Welcome to the confusing land of enharmonics. An enharmonic is a note that has two names, but one sound. The G♭-F♯ example is a perfect example of enharmonics in action. Look at the following chart, which maps out all the notes on the sixth string, fret by fret.

Fret Number	Note	Fret Number	Note
0	E	7	B
1	F	8	C
2	F♯/G♭	9	C♯/D♭
3	G	10	D
4	G♯/A♭	11	D♯/E♭
5	A	12	E
6	A♯/B♭		

Notice that the name of a note with a flat is always one letter higher than the name of the note with a sharp. For instance, F♯/G♭, A♯/B♭, and so on. Most notes have flats and sharps, but there are two exceptions: (1) The interval between B and C is already a half step, so there is no note called B♯, and none called C♭; (2) E and F are also already a half step apart, so, likewise, there are no notes called E♯ or F♭. Technically, E♯ is the same as F, so you can just refer to it as "F." Likewise, B♯ is the same as C, C♭ is B, and F♭ is E—because between each of these is only one half-step. If you can picture a piano keyboard, you'll notice that there is no black key between B and C, or E and F.

Constructing the Major Scale

The major scale is a series of repeating whole and half steps. Every major scale has the same pattern, no matter where you start. This is the reason why you can move the scale shapes around the guitar easily. Theoretically every scale shares the same construction blueprint of half and whole steps. Let's look at the C-Major scale and the intervals between the notes. (See **FIGURE 7-2**.)

FIGURE 7-2 C-Major scale with half and whole steps

| Whole | Whole | Half | Whole | Whole | Whole | Half |

FIGURE 7-3 C-Major scale across one string

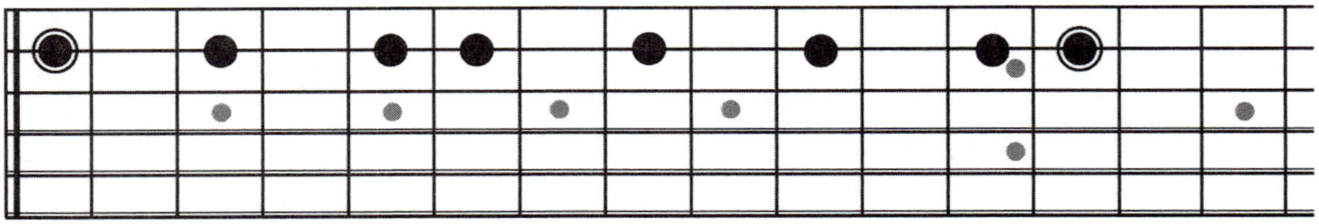

The pattern is whole, whole, half, whole, whole, whole, and half (or W, W, H, W, W, W, H). This is *the* formula for constructing any major scale. Apply this across one string of the guitar so you can really see how the intervals separate. Start on the first fret of the second string. The first fret is C, which is the root of this major scale. Following the formula, move up a whole step (two frets), which puts you on the third fret D. If you follow the pattern all the way up you get a C-Major scale across one string. Look at the neck diagram in **FIGURE 7-3** for the C-Major scale played across one string.

If you look at the scale this way you can see how the pattern repeats—whole steps are two-fret shifts, and half steps are one-fret shifts. Now let's describe the pattern in terms of guitar fret moves. Instead of half step, let's say "up one" and instead of whole step, let's say "up two." So now the pattern is: up two, up two, up one, up two, up two, up two, up one. Start anywhere on the guitar and apply this pattern across a single string. You'll get a perfect major scale. Of course, if you start on a high fret, you'll run out of room on the neck, so start on a lower fret. If your neck continued up forever, the pattern would work no matter where you started.

If the pattern for a major scale never changes, how come the fingerings for scales change on the neck? The guitar is not tuned symmetrically, so depending where you start, and what strings you play on, the scale may change and you play across several strings. If you play the same fingering across one string, you'll always get the same shape.

King Major

In music theory, everything reverts to the good old major scale. Everything that isn't major is some modification of it. So if you understand the major scale and how to spell it, you can figure anything out. Let's look at six basic C-Major scale intervals to see what you can generate from this scale:

C–D (major second)   C–G (perfect fifth)
C–E (major third)   C–A (major sixth)
C–F (perfect fourth)   C–B (major seventh)

The first interval of a scale—a major second—isn't always from C to D as it is in the C-Major scale shown in the previous list. You can locate a major second in any scale if you spell out the scale, find its root, and then find its second note. The same logic applies to any other interval you want to find. For example, if you want to find a major sixth from A, spell out an A-Major scale, find the root note (which would be A), and then find the sixth note of that scale. It's that easy.

Major Rules

Enharmonics can be tricky, so keep these two important points in mind when spelling out major scales and intervals: Scales contain seven different letters (notes) and a letter is never repeated back to back. Just remember, if you're on an F, the next note has to be some form of G, because you must keep moving up the alphabet. Even though F♯ and G♭ are the same note, you'll never see the note of F followed by F♯—in such a case F♯ would be written as G♭ (using the next letter in the alphabet). A lot of these "rules" are conveniences for musicians who read and analyze a lot of music. Musicians are trained to expect certain groupings of notes. When you read music it's much easier to see notes progress to the next pitch if a different letter is used, than if the same note is repeated with a sharp or a flat added. When spelled out, a scale that contains sharps never contains flats, and a scale with flats never contains sharps. For example, the key of A♭ contains the notes A♭, B♭, C, D♭, E♭, F, G, A♭—all flats. The key of A major is spelled A, B, C♯, D, E, F♯, G♯, A—all sharps.

Perfect Sense

The major intervals of seconds, thirds, sixths, and sevenths make sense, but the term "perfect" seems strange. What is so perfect about them? We call them perfect because when you compare C Major and C minor, they both share the same fourth and fifth. Because they don't move, they're called perfect. The other notes with major or minor interval names do shift from scale to scale. Without further ado, let's look at the minor scale and the theory behind it.

Minor Theory

As you learned in the previous section, everything in theory revolves around the major scale. That being the case, one of the easiest ways to construct the minor scale is to think of it as an altered version of major. It's very simple to turn the major scale into minor—just lower the third, sixth, and seventh notes by one half step.

As an example I'll turn a C-Major scale into a C-minor scale. First, I'll identify the notes of C Major and boldface the third, sixth, and seventh notes:

C, D, **E,** F, G, **A, B,** C (C Major)

Now I'll lower those boldface notes one half step.

C, D, **E♭,** F, G, **A♭, B♭,** C, (C minor)

By lowering the third, sixth, and seventh notes in a major scale by one half step, you can easily make a minor scale from any major scale.

FACT

Major and minor scales that share the same root, such as the C-Major scale and C-minor scale, are called "parallel major and minor."

While this method of finding a minor scale is easy, it does require you find the major scale first, and that may not be so easy or efficient. Let's look at a formula for playing minor based on half steps and whole steps. (See **FIGURE 7-4**.)

Just as you can play the major scale across a single string, you can turn the half steps and whole steps into fret moves and play the minor scale across a single string, too; you can really see the separation of the intervals. For a minor scale you have: up two, up one, up two, up two, up one, up two, up two. Apply this across the second string, starting on the first fret C, and you'll come up with **FIGURE 7-5**.

FIGURE 7-4   C-minor scale with half and whole steps

FIGURE 7-5   C-minor scale across one string

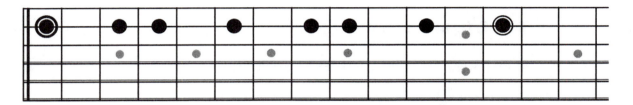

Any theoretical rule that you use for the major scale can be applied to every scale.

Minor Intervals

You already know that the minor scale offers some new intervals—minor third and sixth and seventh. And you also know that the notes that don't change between the two scales are called perfect intervals. There's one catch—look at the intervals of the minor scale:

C–D (major second)
C–E♭ (minor third)
C–F (perfect fourth)
C–G (perfect fifth)
C–A♭ (minor sixth)
C–B♭ (minor seventh)

Notice how the major intervals in our earlier example have changed to minor (the third, sixth, and seventh)? The fourth and fifth are perfect because they stay the same. But notice that the second is still called a major second, rather than a perfect second, even though it did not change between the scales. This is an exception that you just have to memorize. There is a minor second interval, but it's a half step. The major second is a whole step.

QUESTION?

Why is the second interval called "major" instead of "perfect"? The interval didn't change between the major and minor scales, so it seems that it should be called a perfect second. But music theorists have been at this for a long time, and they've settled on "major second" as the name for this interval. Remember, every rule has an exception!

Other Intervals

The other intervals are the diminished interval and augmented interval, neither of which are used extensively in popular music. They're used more for chords and chord theory, which is discussed in the next chapter. But simply, major is usually the larger of the intervals (there is more distance between the notes), and minor is smaller. If you have to get bigger than major, you augment it to make it larger. If you need to get smaller than a minor interval, diminished intervals take care of that. For the actual fingering of these intervals, check out Chapter 16.

Using Theory as You Play

After all this talk you may be wondering where to use all this information. Simply, now you're equipped to really talk about music, and understand licks and examples with greater depth than before.

When you play a lick you can now understand what makes that particular lick work. You can talk about the scale being used, and what notes out of that scale are used most frequently. From that information you can start to devise your own rules for playing what you like. If your favorite guitar player played a D in his solo over a C-minor chord and you absolutely loved that note, figure out how that note relates to the chord below it. Once you've figured out that D is two notes away from the root of the C-minor chord, you can apply that principal to other songs and other chords. You can use seconds over chords, for example. Knowing theory allows you to figure out what you played, and how to repeat it when you want to. No more accidental discoveries that you can't repeat. Music theory can be dry and boring, but if you apply it to your own music and use it to your benefit, it will have meaning to you and it will be very interesting!

Chapter 8

Chords and Chord Progressions

Chords and chord progressions make up the backbone of tonal music. The melody, bass line, guitar parts, and solos are all based on chords and the chord progressions. Understanding chords and their progressions will aid you in all aspects of playing guitar, especially rock and blues.

What Is a Chord?

A chord is defined as three or more notes played simultaneously. But which three? Any three notes? Understanding where chords come from will help you get a thorough grasp on them. Guitarists commonly think of chords as "grips," "boxes," or "shapes." This thinking is convenient to understanding guitar playing, but to understand music, you should know how chords evolved.

In the Old Days . . .

Originally, music was written one line at a time, usually for singers or small instrumental groups. When music evolved to have more than one line sung or played at the same time, people found that certain notes sounded good together, and other notes didn't. As a result, rules were created that stated what intervals could be played together—certain intervals like thirds, fifths, and sixths sounded good together, while other intervals did not. As music evolved into more than two lines played together, certain groupings of notes were commonly found to sound good together. The composers didn't think of chords at this time; what they did think about were individual lines of melody that intersected to form what we know today as chords. If you look back on this old music you can see things that resembled chords. It wasn't until Jean-Philippe Rameau theorized about chords in the eighteenth century that chords were named and understood. But as with all theory, Rameau spoke about chords after they happened, so all he did was name something that already existed.

Triads

Rameau spoke of groupings of notes called triads, which are three-note chords, built in the intervals of thirds. He theorized that triads are formed by stacking or "harmonizing" a major scale together. What he thought in 1722 still holds true today, even in rock and blues music. Chords and harmony come from a harmonized major scale. Let's look at the harmonized C-Major scale in **FIGURE 8-1** to see how triads are formed.

FIGURE 8-1 Harmonized C-Major scale

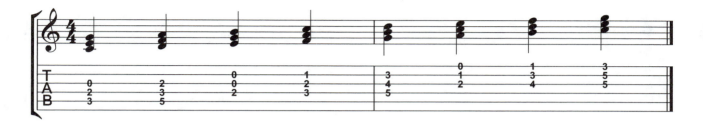

As you can see from the music, these chords are formed by taking notes of the C-Major scale and combining them with other notes from the scale. The method for forming triads is very simple, and if you can draw a major scale, either in music or in letters, you can form triads. Here's an example in letters for you to see how the scale is formed:

STEP 1   Write a C-Major scale on a piece of paper.

C D E F G A B C

STEP 2   Add the interval of a third above each of the notes in the C-Major scale. That is, write E above C, F above D, and so on:

E F G A B C D E
C D E F G A B C

STEP 3   Place thirds again above the line of notes that starts with E. Using notes from the C-Major scale, write G above E, A above F, and so on:

G A B C D E F G
E F G A B C D E
C D E F G A B C

You just formed chords. (Read the chords from bottom to top on vertical rows.) Let's look at the harmonized scale in **FIGURE 8-2**, but this time with the names of the chords.

FIGURE 8-2   Harmonized scale with chord names

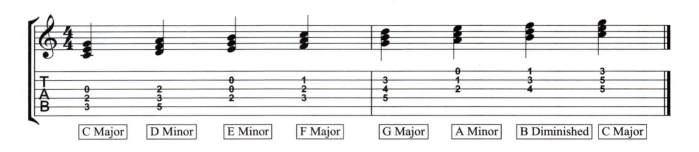

| C Major | D Minor | E Minor | F Major | G Major | A Minor | B Diminished | C Major |

FIGURE 8-3   C-Major chord

TRACK 31

FIGURE 8-4   Familiar C-Major chords

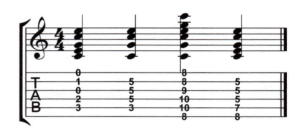

Just by simply arranging the scale in that order you were able to make a lot of chords. Look at the first C-Major chord in **FIGURE 8-3**.

Now as you look at the music and tab, you might say, "That's not the C-Major chord I play." You could be used to playing any of the C-Major chords in **FIGURE 8-4**.

Every one of these chords is a C-Major because each one contains the notes C, E, and G. Some chord shapes, or voicings, contain repeats of the three original notes. But under no circumstances will a C-Major chord ever contain more than three discrete pitches. When you harmonize the scale, you get the basic information about what notes the chords contain, but you won't get chord shapes that look familiar.

Basic Chord Theory

In their simplest form, chords all contain three notes. These notes are referred to as roots, thirds, and fifths, which indicate how far away the intervals are from the root. Take for example a C-Major chord consisting of the notes C, E, G. C is the root, the note E is a third away from C, and G is a fifth away from C. Every interval in a chord is measured away from the root, or name, of the chord. All simple triads contain roots, thirds, and fifths. In the case of a major chord, the triad contains a root, a major third, and a perfect fifth. Look at **FIGURE 8-5** to see the intervals.

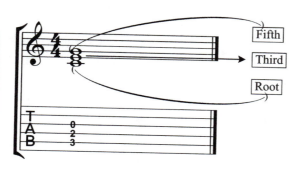

FIGURE 8-5
C-Major triad with intervals

To find a simple major chord, all you have to do is take the first, third, and fifth notes of the major scale that shares the root. For example, to find an E-Major chord, write out the notes of an E-Major scale (E, F♯, G♯, A, B, C♯, D♯, E) and select the first (E), the third (G♯), and the fifth (B). That's an E-Major chord. Try it with a few keys for practice.

Minor Triads

How do you form a minor chord? All you have to do is lower the third one half step (or one fret) of any major chord. Let's use E Major again as an example. The notes for an E-Major triad are E, G♯, B. Using the rule of lowering the third, lower the G♯ to G. Now you have an instant E-minor chord: E, G, B. This works with any chord. Think of your open-position E-Major and E-minor chords—the only finger that changes is the third. You could also spell the minor scale, and play its first, third, and fifth note; either way works. Practice both so your ability to spell scales and chords is strengthened in all facets.

The Other Triads

Classical, jazz, and popular music contain diminished chords. Blues music rarely uses diminished chords, because they are not part of the standard twelve-bar blues progression; however, some rock music does use diminished chords. To make a diminished chord, start with the major chord first and lower the third and fifth. Let's use E again: From E Major (E, G♯, B), lower the G♯ to G and the B to B♭. The notes for an E diminished are E, G, B♭.

The final triad is called an augmented triad. Augmented triads are fairly rare in rock music, although they do come up. (You hear them a lot in jazz and classical music.) An augmented triad is a major triad with a raised fifth. For a C augmented, start with the basic major triad (C, E, G), and raise the fifth G up one half step to G♯, giving you a C-augmented chord (C, E, G♯). Augmented chords do not naturally occur in the harmonized major scale. Nonetheless, they are important to understand.

FACT

Swedish guitarist Yngwie Malmsteen often uses the diminished chord in his music. Frank Zappa and Steve Vai have also used augmented chords.

Chord Progressions

Harmonizing the major scale as shown in **FIGURE 8-1** also gives you the common chords for any given key. In Chapter 2, you learned about the I-IV-V progression and its use in the blues. Remember how you figured the numbering system for the chords? In the blues, you selected only three of the possible seven chords that belong to a key. The example in **FIGURE 8-6** names all the chords in the key of C Major by Roman numeral.

Notice how the Roman numeral system is used to name chords. Uppercase numbers signify major chords, while lowercase numbers signify minor chords. The diminished chord is lowercase with the added degree sign (°). You saw that in the case of blues, referring to chords by numbers was integral to playing the blues progression in every key. Rock music has its standard chord progressions, too. The I-IV-V progression is found in a lot of rock music. If you ever wondered why G, D, and C chords are found in so many songs it's because G, D, and C are part of the harmonized G scale. G is the I chord, C is the IV, and D is the V.

Chords that come from the same key are related and sound good together. Try experimenting with chords from the harmonized scale in your music, and you may find some chord progressions you hadn't though of. Besides the I-IV-V chords, the progression of I-vi-IV-V is used in many older rock songs. **FIGURE 8-7** is a I-vi-IV-V progression in the key of C Major.

FIGURE 8-6   C-Major scale harmonized, with Roman numerals

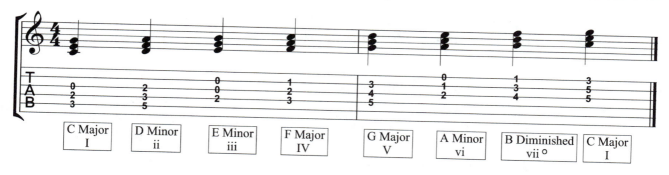

FIGURE 8-7   I-vi-IV-V progression in C Major

TRACK 32

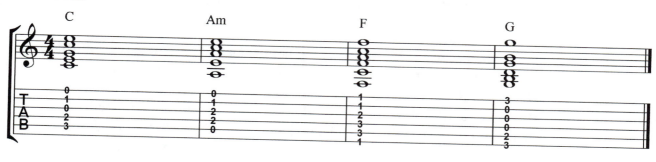

Countless rock songs have used the I-vi-IV-V progression, and here are three:

- "Let It Be" (The Beatles)
- "All My Loving" (The Beatles)
- "In the Still of the Night" (The Five Satins)

The harmonized major scale is just one way to look at chords. It teaches the origin of chords, and while many songs use progressions out of this method, most players do it unknowingly. For many players, a I-IV-V chord progression simply sounds right; they are not aware of its origin and relation to scales.

The music of The Beatles is a wonderful place to start studying and analyzing chord progressions, because many of their songs use progressions from harmonized scales.

The important thing to remember is that theory isn't the only way. It's just another tool for you to use—something to get the job done. Many students are baffled when their favorite band's chord progressions don't come from any perceivable scale. This is fine. Music doesn't have to relate. The most important thing in the end is how the music sounds. If you like the sound, then it is good and valid. If theory doesn't work and you can't number the chords, don't worry!

Chord Families and Tall Chords

The next step is to learn extended chords. Extended chords are chords that contain additional notes on top of the normal triads. Western music is based on a system of tonality called tertian harmony because all the chords are based on the interval of a third. A third interval is between the root and the third, and another third interval is between the third and the fifth. The third interval is the essential building block of chords and harmony.

To extend chords beyond their basic three-note structures, you simply add another third on top. Just as you did in the previous example, you use only notes from the parent scale. When you use only notes from one scale to make chords you are using that scale "diatonically," which means "from the scale." Because extended chords contain four or more notes, they are commonly referred to as tall chords, because they occupy more of the staff than simple chords do.

Seventh Chords

When we harmonized the scale again, we created seventh chords. Why seventh chords? Because the highest note in each chord is seven notes away from the root. Chord names are very literal, even though they can sound like calculus coordinates. Look at **FIGURE 8-8** showing the C-Major scale harmonized in sevenths.

From this figure you form a bunch of new chords: major seventh, minor seventh, half-diminished seventh, and dominant seventh. Tab was not included with this figure because these chords are not playable on guitar. Due to the guitar's tuning, not all combinations of notes are possible; you also only have four fingers. **FIGURE 8-9** shows the same harmonized scale, but this time guitar–friendly (or idiomatic) voicings are used in the notation and the tab.

The notes in these chords are the same as in **FIGURE 8-8**; however, the order of the notes has been shifted around. When you play these chords, realize that you haven't left C Major; all the chords are based on combinations of notes from the C-Major scale, again diatonic notes. Try substituting seventh chords for the simple triads you may be already playing. For instance, in your I-vi-IV-V song, you can use the same numbers; just substitute the new seventh chords.

FIGURE 8-8   C-Major scale harmonized in seventh chords

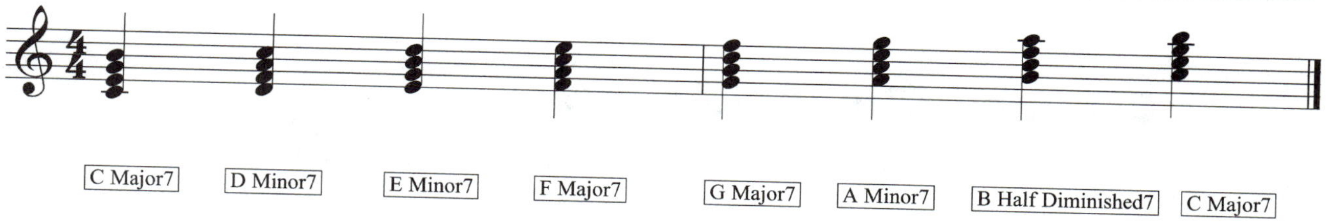

| C Major7 | D Minor7 | E Minor7 | F Major7 | G Major7 | A Minor7 | B Half Diminished7 | C Major7 |

FIGURE 8-9 Idiomatic guitar voicing for seventh chords

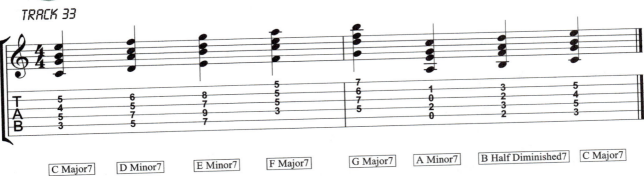

Modern rock bands like Incubus and the Foo Fighters have used extended seventh chords in their music. Pink Floyd has also used extended chords in their music.

How to Read Chord Symbols

Now that you can play a few extended chords, let's look at examples of how extended chords are written in music:

- Major seventh chords are written as: CM7, Cmaj7, Cmajor7, or C$^{\Delta}$7.
- Minor seventh chords are written as: Cm7, Cmin7, Cminor7, or C-7.
- Dominant seventh chords are written as: G7 or Gdom7. If there's just a letter and the number 7, you know it's a dominant seventh chord.
- Full-diminished chords (less commonly found in rock and blues) are written as C°7. If you don't see the number seven after the degree sign, it's just a simple triad.
- Half-diminished chords are written as: C$^{\emptyset}$7. The normal diminished circle is cut in half.

Common Chord Voicings

There are some nice moveable chord shapes for these extended chords that you should learn. If you have a chance to play in a school-sponsored band, either jazz or pit musical, knowing these chord shapes is vital; all you see is chord symbols, never little box diagrams. **FIGURE 8-10** is a chart of the basic chords broken down by category. All these shapes are moveable, and at least one example is given with a root on the sixth, fifth, and the fourth strings.

FIGURE 8-10   Common seventh chord shapes

G7
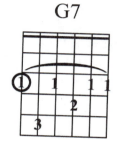

C7
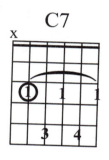

G Min7
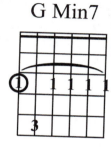

C Min7
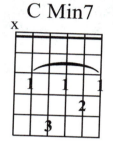

Gmaj7
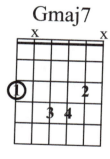

C Maj7
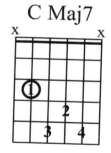

G Dim7
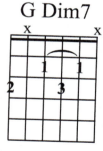

C Dim7
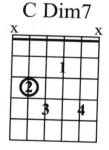

G ∅
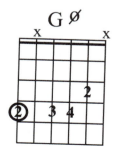

G ∅
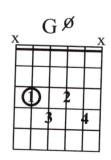

Suspended Chords

A very popular chord is the suspended chord, which is commonly referred to as a "sus" chord. Simply, a suspended chord is any triad that suspends the third and replaces it with either the second or fourth note of the scale. Usually the music indicates which one it requires, but if you just see "Csus," you can use either the fourth or the second in place of the third. **FIGURE 8-11** shows some very common suspended chords.

FIGURE 8-11
Suspended chord shapes

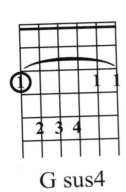

G sus4

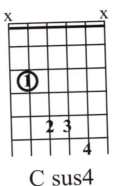

C sus4

Since suspended chords lack the third of a chord, they are neither major nor minor—they fall into the same category as the power chords you studied in Chapter 2, which also lack thirds. Lacking a third makes chords somewhat ambiguous and open.

Extended Chord Theory

All these chords start with the same basic triads you learned earlier and added another note on top. Two factors affect the naming process: the type of original chord (major, minor, or diminished), and the distance of the top note. Here's a list of the various seventh chords found in music.

- **Major seventh:** A Major triad with a major seventh added to it
- **Minor seventh:** A minor triad with a minor seventh added to it
- **Dominant seventh:** A Major triad with a minor seventh added to it
- **Half-diminished seventh:** A diminished triad with a minor seventh added to it
- **Full-diminished seventh:** A diminished triad with a diminished seventh added to it

Getting Even Taller

Chords can be built taller than sevenths. Actually, chords can be built in ninths, elevenths, and thirteenths. If you keep placing thirds on top of the original chord progression diatonically, you keep building up the chords. Chords like these are always named from the highest note present. If you're interested in such chords, refer to Appendix A to find some great books pertaining to chords. Getting beyond basic seventh chords could take a whole book to explain, and starts looking a lot like jazz, so this is as far as we'll go. As for rock and blues music, these are the common chords you find. But great players are always coming up with new chords. Chords can take a lifetime to master, but if you can learn all these voicings and recognize where to use them, you've come a long way.

Test Yourself

FIGURE 8-12 is a short eight-measure test using seventh chord symbols. Read through it using the new chord symbols, without looking ahead to the solution, which follows in **FIGURE 8-13**.

FIGURE 8-12   Chord chart test

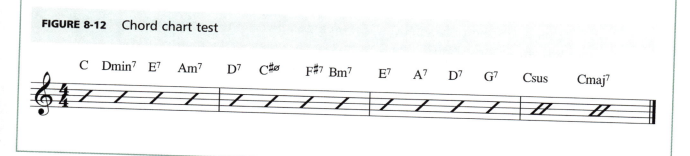

FIGURE 8-13   Chord chart solutions

TRACK 34

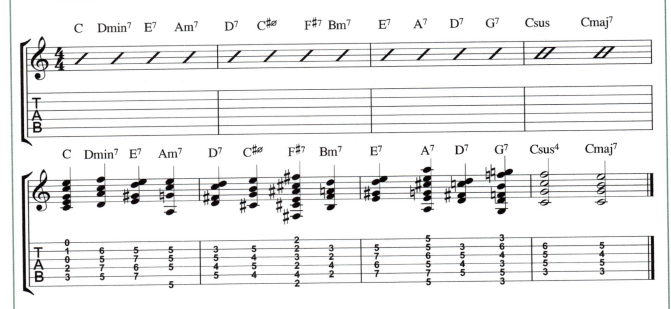

This is not the only solution; if you came up with the correct chords on different strings you still got it right. Give ten players the same chart, and you may get ten different but correct answers!

FIGURE 8-14   Blues with dominant chords

TRACK 35

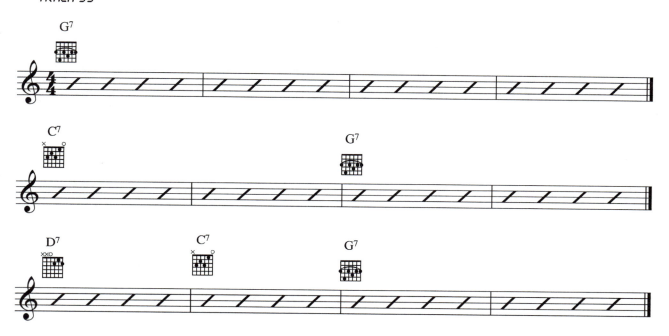

The Blues Chords

The blues also frequently uses dominant seventh chords in place of the normal major triads. Instead of C, F, G, for a C blues, you can use C7, F7, G7. **FIGURE 8-14** is an example of a twelve-bar blues using dominant seventh chords.

In blues, only dominant seventh chords work; major sevenths sound very strange and out of place. Try incorporating these new chords into your blues playing to spice up your rhythm playing.

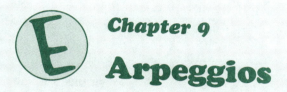

Chapter 9

Arpeggios

The name may sound grandiose, but an arpeggio is simply a chord played one note at a time. Arpeggios are also referred to as frozen chords. This chapter looks at what you need to know to master them as a tool in your repertoire.

The Theory of Arpeggios

You've played many arpeggios in your life without even realizing it. The intro to "Stairway to Heaven"? That's an arpeggio. The opening to "Freebird" is all arpeggios. Any time you finger-pick through a chord or play a chord slowly, you're playing an arpeggio. An arpeggio shares the exact same notes as a chord, but you vary the timing of each note. It's the presentation that differs here: one note at a time versus all at once.

FIGURE 9-1
C-Major
arpeggio

Let's look at a simple example of an arpeggio (see **FIGURE 9-1**). Take the notes of a C-Major chord (C, E, G) and instead of playing them in your familiar chord shape, play them one note at a time. There's really nothing special going on here, nothing radical or new. But when done right, you won't know what hit you! Take a look at the example in **FIGURE 9-2** of arpeggios over a I-vi-IV-V progression in the key of C.

You may not believe it to hear it, but all the notes in that example directly coincide with the notes in the chords. The example is laid out with one measure per chord (four measures in total). For each measure, you've taken the notes of the chords and spelled them out one by one.

FIGURE 9-2   Arpeggios over a I-vi-IV-V progression

TRACK 36

One of the greatest examples of arpeggios is in the Eagles song "Hotel California." The famous two-guitar lead at the end of the solo is comprised entirely of arpeggios. The arpeggios are taken from the same repeating chord progression that is used throughout the song.

Becoming Aware

It happens to every guitar player at a certain point—you become aware. You become aware of chords, you become aware of scales, and, in general, you become aware of how other guitar players create solos and riffs. This is akin to finding out that there's a secret camera on you at all times; all of a sudden it really matters what you say and do.

For players early in their guitar-playing experiences, it's okay to just crank away at the blues scale, riffing endlessly without knowing or caring too much about the smaller details. But for guitar students, a real cathartic moment comes when they become aware of chords and their relationship to everything else in music. Simply put, chords rule everything. Chords dictate what notes can be in the melody, what notes are in the bass lines, and what tones sound good in a solo. Chords have a lot of power. Once you become aware of them, it's hard to ignore them.

Chord Dictatorship

Chords are like questions. When you play a C-Major chord you expect a certain answer—notes from that chord or scale. When a chord is played, the notes from that chord become the strongest notes to improvise melodies with. For any given chord you play over, the notes in those chords are the best and most direct choices. If you play a C-Major chord, the notes C, E, and G sound the best. They sound good because they're played in the chord, and you are merely reiterating them.

The Big Picture

As you can see, the relationship between chords and music is undeniable. When most singers create a melody, they do so over pre-existing chords. If you went back and compared any melody line to the chords, you'd find that the melody line utilizes notes from those chords.

If music ignored the chords totally, it wouldn't sound very good. This interaction between chords and melodies is vital to tonal music.

Arpeggios are usually played in order, meaning that the notes follow their usual order, unlike normal guitar chords that shuffle the notes around for convenience. Basic arpeggios are only three or four notes long, and unless you repeated them in different octaves, any examples I gave would be very short. Since arpeggios correlate with the chords, we will look at major, minor, and diminished arpeggio fingerings. Augmented arpeggios will be left out because they're used so seldom, but don't let that stop you from trying them on your own!

Fingerings for Major Arpeggios

To form major arpeggio fingerings, all you need to do is identify the notes of a major chord and play them one after another. Let's use G Major this time for variety. The notes of a G-Major chord are G, B, D. Look at the notes G, B, D over the entire fingerboard in the full neck diagram in **FIGURE 9-3** of a G-Major arpeggio.

Again, looking at the whole neck like this can be a little intimidating, but we can distill this information into some moveable shapes. In **FIGURE 9-4**, the first shape starts with a root on the sixth string. Just as in the major scales, this shape begins on a second finger.

There is an alternate fingering for this arpeggio that starts with the second finger. See **FIGURE 9-5**.

FIGURE 9-3   G-Major arpeggio full neck diagram

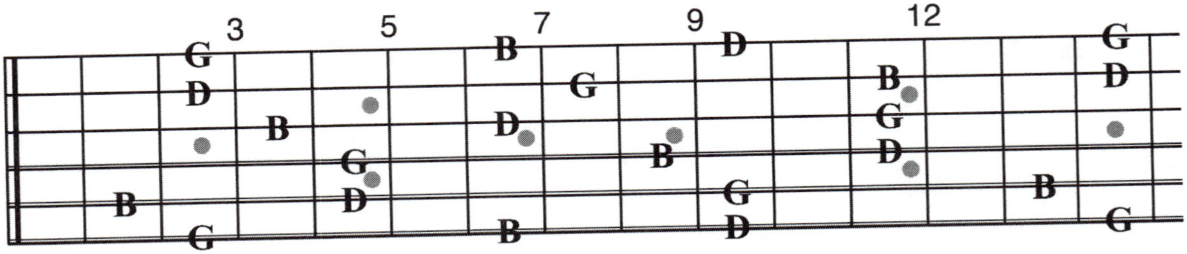

FIGURE 9-4   G-Major arpeggio root on sixth string

FIGURE 9-5   G-Major arpeggio alternate fingering

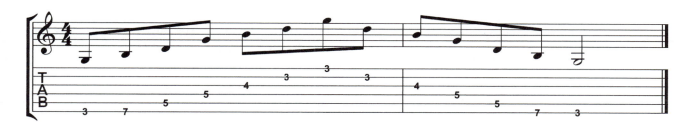

FIGURE 9-6   G-Major arpeggio root on the fifth string

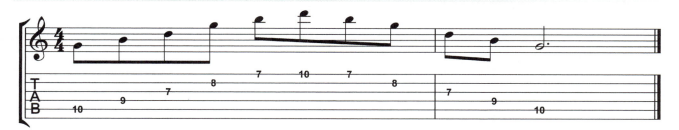

FIGURE 9-7   G-Major arpeggio alternate fingering on the fifth string

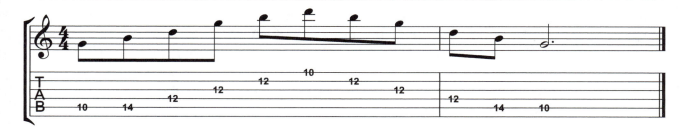

FIGURE 9-8 G-Major arpeggio, long fingering

TRACK 37

While there may be common fingerings for these arpeggios, choose the fingering that is the most comfortable for you. As you move to the fifth string, there are two arpeggio shapes, one from the pinky finger and one from the first finger. **FIGURES 9-6** and **9-7** share the same notes, but finger shapes change; we've seen this happen often in scales and chords.

These four shapes constitute the most typical and comfortable shapes on the guitar, but don't let this stop you from exploring the neck. Any combination of G, B, D will make a G-Major arpeggio. **FIGURE 9-8** is an unorthodox fingering that spans many frets and traverses the neck.

Fingerings for Minor Arpeggios

Minor arpeggios get their tones from minor chords. To turn a G-Major chord into a G-minor chord, all you have to do is lower the third note from B to B♭. The same holds true for arpeggios: To transform the major arpeggios to minor arpeggios, you lower B to B♭. Doing so changes the shapes completely, but that's okay—only one note changes, so they don't look that different. For the sixth string, you get only one fingering shape; this one starts with the first finger. See **FIGURE 9-9**.

For the fifth string, there are two fingerings, and like major arpeggios they start with the first and fourth fingers, and both contain the exact same notes. Choose the shape that feels more comfortable to play. See **FIGURES 9-10** and **9-11**.

FIGURE 9-9 G-minor arpeggio root on the sixth string

FIGURE 9-10 G-minor arpeggio root on the fifth string

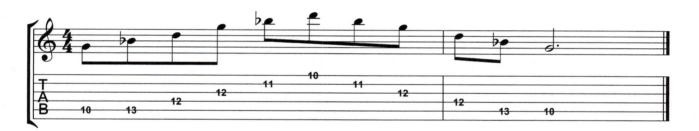

FIGURE 9-11 G-minor arpeggio alternate fingering root on the fifth string

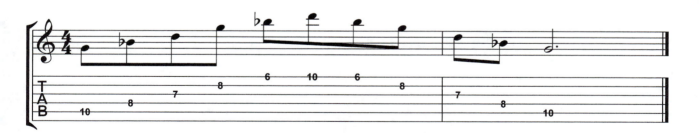

FIGURE 9-12   G-Minor arpeggio, long fingering

TRACK 38

You can also do a long arching lick (as shown in **FIGURE 9-8**) in minor, by simply changing the Bs to B♭s. **FIGURE 9-12** shows the long arpeggio fingering for minor.

Fingerings for Diminished Arpeggios

Approaching the diminished arpeggio requires a slightly different tack than with major and minor. The diminished triad is not used much, therefore, the examples here are based on the diminished seventh chord. A G-diminished seventh triad is spelled G, B♭, D♭, E. All diminished seventh chords share one very special trait: They are symmetrical. The distance between each of the notes is a minor third; no arpeggios we've studied thus far have had this symmetrical relationship. Symmetrical shapes are a

FIGURE 9-13   G-diminished seventh arpeggio

TRACK 39

FIGURE 9-14   G-diminished pattern shifted up

lot of fun on guitar, because their fingerings repeat. Let's look at what symmetrical looks like on guitar. The basic fingering for a G-diminished seventh arpeggio is shown in **FIGURE 9-13**.

Now you can take this exact finger shape, and move it up the same string three frets higher, and you will still be playing G-diminished seventh. Try playing **FIGURE 9-14**.

You can keep moving this pattern up three frets, and you will always be playing G-diminished seventh. It's extremely easy to play diminished, because the fingerings across the neck are all the same. If you need to move this into other keys, just look where the circled finger is to find the root. You can move that finger to any root you need and repeat the process up every three frets.

There's another shape that utilizes some lower strings that you can move the same way. **FIGURE 9-15** utilizes a G-diminished shape on the second, third, and fourth strings.

FIGURE 9-15   G-diminished seventh arpeggio on inside strings

FIGURE 9-16   G-diminished seventh arpeggio across all strings

TRACK 40

You can shift this shape up the neck as well; just move up three frets and the pattern repeats.

There are some shapes that utilize simpler fingerings. Look at **FIGURE 9-16** that starts on the sixth string and moves across the neck all the way up to the high string.

To hear diminished arpeggios in rock music, listen to Ritchie Blackmore of Deep Purple and Yngwie Malmsteen. If you'd like to go to the source, J.S. Bach is a great place to start. Check out his sonatas and partitas for solo violin.

Applying Arpeggios

Enough talk about shapes and such! You're ready to apply this to music. Let's invent a chord progression using simple open-position chords to play arpeggios over. Let's use this simple chord progression in the key of C Major: C Major, A minor, F Major, G Major, E minor, D minor, C Major. Play through that cycle of chords and get the sound in your head. To make an arpeggio solo, all we have to do is move the shapes we learned earlier to the correct roots. For the example in **FIGURE 9-17**, use only shapes with roots on the fifth strings.

It's amazing what you can do with these shapes, and they sound so good! **FIGURE 9-18** shows another example utilizing just two chords, A minor and B-diminished seventh.

FIGURE 9-17 Arpeggio, example one

TRACK 41

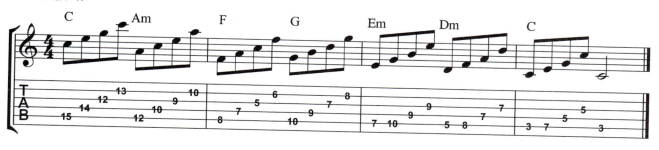

FIGURE 9-18 Arpeggio, example two

TRACK 42

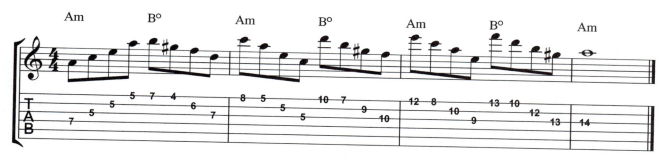

As you can see from these two examples, making your own fingerings isn't that difficult, but it does mean that you have to know what chords you're playing over. Until you have a lot of experience, you probably won't be whipping these out on the spur of the moment; many of your arpeggio solos will be planned, and that's just fine! There's nothing wrong with working things out in advance; you have to crawl before you walk.

Other Arpeggios

Since an arpeggio is nothing more than a chord frozen, do you have to limit your arpeggio options to just simple triads? Of course not! Some of the most beautiful chords on the guitar have extra notes on them.

FIGURE 9-19   Chord progression using added ninths

FIGURE 9-19 is a great chord progression using added-ninth chords.

How would you create an arpeggio pattern for C Major added ninth and A minor added ninth? Simple: figure out what the extra note is and fit it into your arpeggio shape. For C Major, the ninth is D. Add that into your arpeggio shape, and you come up with **FIGURE 9-20**.

For the A-minor ninth chord, the ninth is B. You can also add that into the shape to come up with **FIGURE 9-21**.

You can combine these shapes into a run and come up with a very cool lick. Again, a little brainpower goes a long way here. See **FIGURE 9-22**.

FIGURE 9-20   C Major added-ninth arpeggio

FIGURE 9-21   A-minor added-ninth arpeggio

FIGURE 9-22   Added-ninth arpeggios combined

TRACK 43

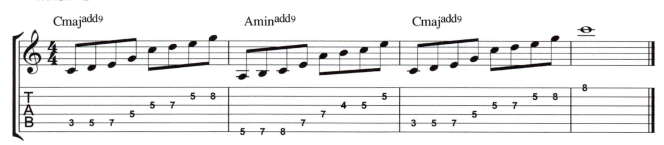

Arpeggios in the Blues Progression

The blues isn't just the blues scale. True blues playing is a conglomeration of scales and arpeggios used freely. Trying to talk about the elements separately is difficult, because when you hear a great player you hear the finished product, not the process the player learned. Since you know that the blues progression is built from three chords, you can take those chords and make them into arpeggios. **FIGURE 9-23** shows an example of the twelve-bar blues progression in F using nothing but triads for the chords.

FIGURE 9-23   Twelve-bar F blues using arpeggios

TRACK 44

As you can hear, all of these notes sound great over the chords. But in reality no blues player plays just arpeggios; he or she incorporates many different things to make solos. Use this as a guide to what's available to play, and try mixing scales and arpeggios into great blues solos.

FACT

Players who use arpeggios include Steve Vai, Joe Satriani, Yngwie Malmsteen, Joe Walsh, Don Felder, Trey Anastasio, and John Petrucci.

The best way to practice this material is to apply it to real music. Take sample chord progressions from songs and try to create arpeggio lines with them. Make up your own chord progressions as exercises and work them out. For you blues players, work through the blues progression in different keys—especially A and E. The more work you do on this the better you will know the material. And most important, study solos you like. You may not "get" what arpeggios are really about until you hear an experienced player use them. If you like the more modern technical players like Vai, Satriani, and Malmsteen, then you've heard arpeggios a lot of the time. Blues players use arpeggios all the time, but they're harder to spot; they may use one or two notes from an arpeggio and then move on to something else. But in the end the result is music, and to speak the language of music well you have to be versed in all aspects of musical vocabulary. Arpeggios are just one more trick in your bag. Ⓔ

Chapter 10

Modes

At some point everyone has heard the term "modes," yet few know what they really are or what they can do for your playing. Modes were first used in ancient Greek music, and reappeared in Gregorian chant. After the end of chant, modes disappeared until the nineteenth century when they became popular again. A mode is just another kind of scale, but it lies hidden in the major scale we all know and love, yearning to break free. Now you can learn how to take modes off your "to do" list and put them into your playing.

Modes Defined

You can think of a mode as a displaced scale. For instance, what would happen if you took all the notes from C Major (no sharps or flats) but instead of starting and ending on C, you started on D and ended on D? Would it still be C Major? No, you would be playing a mode, even though you were using the notes of C. In this way a mode is a displaced scale. You can play a major scale starting on other points than the root. Since there are seven notes in the scale, there are seven modes; one starting from each tone. The result is seven new scales, each with its own name. In this chapter I'll describe modes and how to find them by using examples from the C-Major scale; but understand that modes can be based on other major scales, as well.

The Mode You Already Know—Ionian

The first mode is the simplest mode to deal with: it's the major scale. Even though we've been saying "major scale" for quite some time, it's also known by the Greek term "Ionian mode." Every mode has a Greek name because the Greeks named them. Since you studied the major scale extensively already, there's no need to repeat the fingering here. Just know that the Ionian mode and the major scale are the same thing.

The Second Mode—Dorian

When you play a major scale starting on the second note and ending on the same second note one octave higher, you form a new scale called the Dorian mode. Using the C-Major scale as an example, when it starts on the second note D, the scale is called D Dorian because it starts on D; and it's called the second mode because D is the second note on the C-Major scale. For the modes discussed in this book, I'll give the two most common and useful fingerings for each one. Each is two octaves long, one starting on the sixth string and one on the fifth string.

The Dorian mode is actually a scale by itself and doesn't have to be tied to a parent scale. It's actually quite difficult to discuss modes in relation to parent scales because you have to think backwards to find out where they come from, which can be tedious. When you look at the notes of the D-Dorian mode (D, E, F, G, A, B, C), you may notice that it greatly resembles a D-minor scale (D, E, F, G, A, B♭, C). The difference is that in the D-Dorian mode, the note B is not a B♭ as it is in the D-minor scale. All the other notes are the same. Because it's so close to being D minor, we can describe D Dorian as a minor mode with a raised sixth note. That really is the simplest way to think about modes—altered major and minor scales—rather than thinking about where they come from. So the formula for Dorian is: Start with the minor scale and raise the sixth tone one half step. Now you can make the fingerings simply by taking the two-octave minor scale fingerings and raising the sixth note one half step. To form the D Dorian from the sixth string you get **FIGURE 10-1**. From the fifth string you end up with **FIGURE 10-2**.

FIGURE 10-1   D-Dorian sixth string root

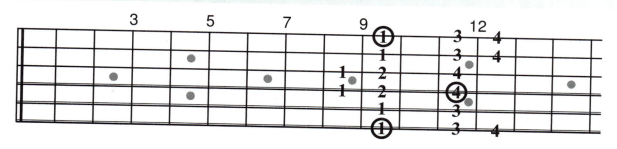

FIGURE 10-2   D-Dorian fifth string root

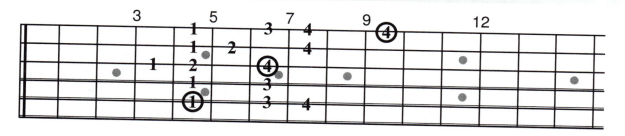

As you can see, the D-Dorian mode is almost exactly like a D-minor scale, which helps illustrate that you can use the Dorian mode in place of a minor scale. That raised sixth tone gives you a little color and uniqueness that you normally don't hear in the world of plain major and minor. Modes are like flavors: Major and minor are vanilla and chocolate, and modes are the more exotic flavors. Try recording yourself playing a D-minor chord and play the D-Dorian mode over it to see if you like it. "Moondance" by Van Morrison is a popular tune that is based on the Dorian mode.

ALERT!

All of the mode shapes presented in this chapter are based on moveable scale shapes. Even though I discuss modes only from C Major, you can move the shapes around the same way you moved them in other chapters.

The Third Mode—Phrygian

Using the C-Major scale as an example, when you play that scale from its third note and complete it you get the E-Phrygian mode. The notes of this mode are E, F, G, A, B, C, D. As a scale, this resembles E minor (E, F♯, G, A, B, C, D); the only difference is that the F♯ is lowered to F. So, you can say the Phrygian mode is a minor mode with the second tone lowered one half step. Using the minor scale fingerings, you just lower the second note one fret. **FIGURE 10-3** shows E Phrygian with a root on the sixth string.

You do the same to the fifth string fingering in **FIGURE 10-4**, lowering the second note one fret.

Because the modes refer to specific tones in the major and minor scales, start thinking about the numbers of the scale tones as you play them. When you practice, be aware of what number you're on.

Since Phrygian is a minor type mode, you can use it anywhere a minor scale would work. The Phrygian mode is frequently used in the music of Spain, so you may have a tinge of "Spanish" color to the scale. Because of its association with the music of Spain, this mode is less

FIGURE 10-3   E-Phrygian root on the sixth string

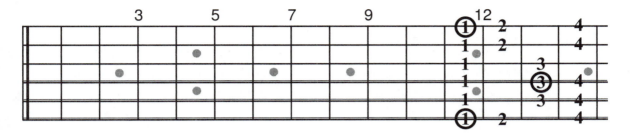

FIGURE 10-4   E-Phrygian root on the fifth string

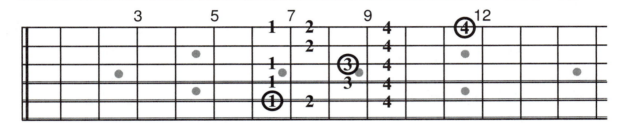

frequently used in modern music, but it does come in handy, so learn it and use it when you feel it fits.

The Fourth Mode—Lydian

As you're starting to see, there's a new mode for each tone you start on. Each mode is described from what note (first, second, third, and so on) it starts on. From now on, it will just be understood that the fourth mode starts on the fourth note and so on. Again, using the C-Major scale, the F-Lydian mode consists of the notes F, G, A, B, C, D, E. It resembles a major scale with a raised fourth pitch. F Major consists of F, G, A, B♭, C, D, E, and F-Lydian raises the B♭ to B. To make a Lydian mode from any note, all you have to do is think of the major scale, then raise the fourth note one half step up, or one fret up. **FIGURE 10-5** shows the F-Lydian mode on the sixth string: **FIGURE 10-6** shows the F-Lydian mode with a root on the fifth string.

The Lydian mode has a unique character to it, because it goes beyond the normal "happy" characteristics of major scales. Because of its unique sound, Lydian has long been a favorite of TV and film composers: just watch the Discovery Channel, you'll hear *lots* of Lydian. In rock music, Frank Zappa and Steve Vai are big fans of the Lydian mode and use it often in their music. This is a great alternative to a regular major scale, which can sound a little bland.

The Fifth Mode—Mixolydian

The Mixolydian mode is a major mode that, on the C-Major scale, starts on G and resembles a G-Major scale with a lowered seventh tone. This is

FIGURE 10-5   F-Lydian mode sixth string root

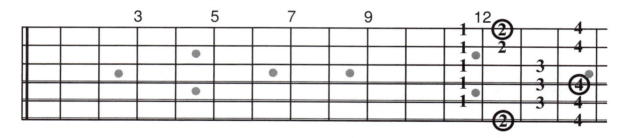

FIGURE 10-6   F-Lydian mode root on the fifth string

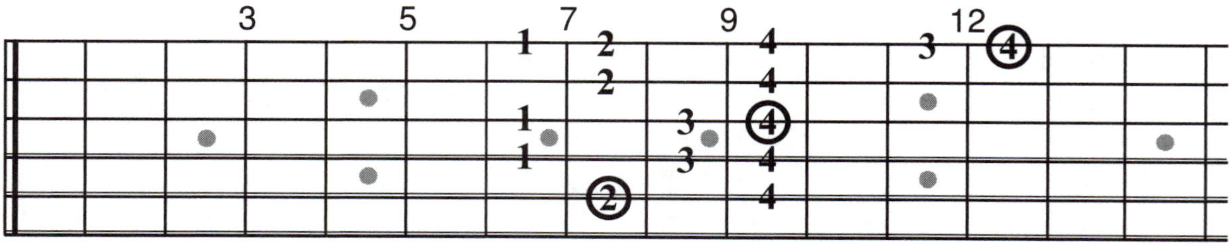

the most useful mode for rock and blues guitar playing. The formula for G-Mixolydian is major B seventh. **FIGURE 10-7** shows the fingerings to the G-Mixolydian mode starting on the sixth.

Notice how the shape looks a lot like a major scale, with one finger changed? That's a characteristic of most modes. **FIGURE 10-8** shows the fingering for the fifth string root of G-Mixolydian.

The reason this mode is so useful is that it's a good replacement for the pentatonic scale in blues playing. The Mixolydian mode still gives you most of the color of the pentatonic scale, but also gives you more tones to work with. This mode is also the first chord that directly links up with the dominant seventh chord, a staple of rock and blues playing. Remember the dominant seventh chords (G seventh and C seventh)? The Mixolydian mode is a perfect match for those chords. If you compare the notes of G seventh to the G-Mixolydian mode you can see that the mode has all the notes of the chord. By playing the

FIGURE 10-7   G-Mixolydian mode sixth string root

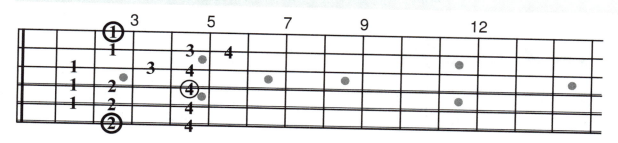

FIGURE 10-8   G-Mixolydian mode fifth string root

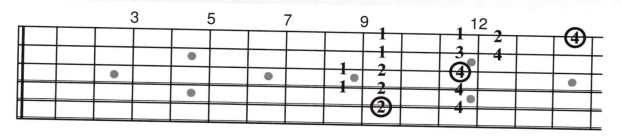

G Mixolydian mode against a G7 chord, you'll be hitting every important note!

G Mixolydian **G** A **B** C **D** E **F**
G Seventh   **G B D F**

The Sixth Mode—Aeolian

The sixth mode of the major scale is the Aeolian mode, which is the second-easiest mode to understand. "Aeolian" is the name for the minor scale, just as "Ionian" is a fancy name for major scale. Remember, every time you play a minor scale, you're using the notes of a major scale to do so. If you recall from Chapter 3, the major and minor pentatonic scales have the same shape but start in different parts of the scale. That's because they share the same notes and are modes of each other, in the same way that C Major and A minor have the exact same notes yet sound different. If this example doesn't sell you on modes, nothing will!

You already know the fingerings, but if you forget, refer to Chapter 6.

The Seventh Mode—Locrian

Locrian is a strange mode; it's the "ugly duckling" mode in a way. It's very rarely played in rock and blues music because of its odd construction. Locrian is a minor mode with a lowered second and a lowered fifth. Remember learning that fifths are perfect and never changed? Here's the exception: Locrian makes the fifth one half step lower. This is one reason why this mode is less attractive to play. But don't let that stop you; check out the fingerings. You could be the first brave guitarist to find a good use for this mode. Although Phrygian is a minor mode with a lowered second tone, Locrian adds the lowered fifth as well. The fingerings for the B-Locrian mode from the sixth string are shown in **FIGURE 10-9**.

FIGURE 10-9 B-Locrian mode sixth string root

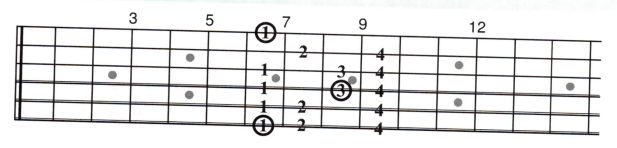

FIGURE 10-10 B-Locrian mode fifth string root

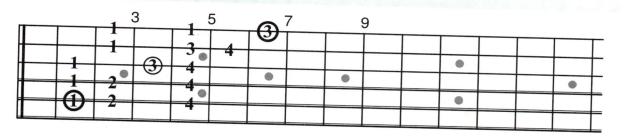

Playing it, you can really hear how dark and unusual it sounds. Metallica found a great use for the Locrian mode—their song "Wherever I May Roam" uses the Locrian mode for the main riff.

The fingering for the B-Locrian mode fifth string root is shown in **FIGURE 10-10**.

A clever way to remember the modes in order, from first mode through seventh mode, is to think of the sentence: "I Don't Play Lame Music Any Longer." The first letter of each word corresponds with the first letter of the mode's name.

Applying Modes to Your Playing

Learning this stuff is all well and good for your brain, but if you can't apply it to real situations, it will never mean much to you. So, let's talk about the useful modes. You already know the Ionian and Aeolian modes (the basic major and minor scales). Of the remaining five, only Dorian, Lydian, and Mixolydian are really vital to learn. Not that Phrygian and Locrian aren't great modes; it's just that they lack the everyday uses the others have.

Uses of Dorian

Back in Chapter 5, you stumbled upon this mode by accident. You added tones to the pentatonic and all of a sudden Dorian just emerged. Dorian works really well in place of the minor pentatonic. It will give you more spice than a normal minor scale will, and that raised sixth is a beautiful note that stands out. **FIGURE 10-11** is a nice lick using A Dorian that you can throw into any A blues with confidence, because A Dorian can substitute for A-minor pentatonic.

In addition to being a great replacement for the blues scale, Dorian must be used in some situations. Two well-known Dorian tunes are "Oye Como Va" by Carlos Santana and "Breathe" by Pink Floyd. Those are situations where other scales, such as minor or pentatonic, won't sound

 FIGURE 10-11 A Dorian example

TRACK 45

right. Another way to look at modes is to realize that there is only one note different about them compared to normal scales. A Dorian is the same as A minor, except it has an F♯ instead of an F. So with that in mind, you're really playing A Dorian when you play F♯ over an A-minor chord. Any other note could be A minor—F♯ is the only distinguishing feature.

Uses of Lydian

The Lydian mode can be used as a direct replacement for the major scale. If major sounds too tame for you, then Lydian is a good choice. **FIGURE 10-12** shows a nice C-Lydian example that repeats in a few spots on the neck.

Again, this mode is different from the C-Major scale only if you play the raised fourth. All the other notes could be C Major; only the raised fourth tells you for sure that you are in C-Lydian. A great Lydian song is Joe Satriani's "Flying in a Blue Dream."

Uses for Mixolydian

Mixolydian is a very useful mode for rock and blues players. Countless songs have been written using this mode, so out of all the new modes, this is the one to spend the most time with. Mixolydian can be a great major scale replacement, but it really shines when it comes to the blues. The blues typically uses either major chords or dominant seventh chords,

FIGURE 10-12   C-Lydian example

TRACK 46

FIGURE 10-13 C-Mixolydian example

TRACK 47

and the Mixolydian mode is the only scale (besides the blues scale and the pentatonic) that hits all the notes of a dominant seventh chord. Some players have even called Mixolydian the dominant mode. **FIGURE 10-13** is a nice example of a C-Mixolydian mode, perfect for C blues.

Because of its uses in the blues, you'll come back to this scale again and again. As with every mode you've learned, the lowered seventh note is the only distinguishing factor. Otherwise, it's just a plain major scale. So if you're trying to play Mixolydian you need to hit the lowered seventh a lot. A great Mixolydian song is "Sweet Home Alabama" by Lynyrd Skynyrd.

General Modal Uses

Modes really work well over one chord vamps. A vamp is played by repeating one chord for a long time. When there's only one chord, you can have fun and experiment with different sounds and colors. For example if you're playing over just a C-Major chord, you could play any of the major modes: C Ionian, C Lydian, or C Mixolydian. The same holds true for minor. Try Dorian, Phrygian, Aeolian, or Locrian. "Jam bands," like the Grateful Dead, Phish, and Aquarium Rescue Unit often jam on long, one- or two-chord vamps. It's no surprise that their guitar players frequently use modes in these contexts.

Playing modes will really start to separate you from the average pentatonic-box player. As you get familiar with them, try to utilize them in your soloing and writing. Modes can be great tools for improvising, so have fun and explore the new sounds you can now create. Ⓔ

Chapter 11
Technique

Technique refers to how you use your body to play guitar, and it's one of the few things in guitar playing for which there is a right and wrong. Using your body properly allows you to improve your playing and develop the speed and facility that are the result of good technique. This chapter explains the interaction between your body and muscles and the guitar, and gives you tips on how you can improve your technique.

Why Technique Matters

Technique, chops, speed, or whatever you want to call it, is an essential part of playing any instrument. While there are different styles of guitar, all require good technique. For instance, if you plan on playing jazz guitar you'd better get your hands in shape because jazz music demands fast playing from time to time. Classical music is another example where you have to have developed a lot of facility with your hands to play well.

Have you ever watched a video of your favorite player and said, "It looks so easy," because the notes just seem to stream effortlessly from the player's hands? It looks easy because it *is* easy to that player. You've probably also seen some less experienced players who make the process look very difficult. The whole point of good technique is playing effortlessly, no matter how slow or fast you play. Many players equate technique with speed, but speed is just a byproduct of great technique.

FACT

In different decades, guitar technique has taken different twists. In the 1980s, there was an explosion of "shredders" who reinvented what could be played on the guitar. These players pushed the boundaries of guitar playing to places never before dreamed of. These guys played faster than anyone had previously, so fast that they "shredded" the notes to pieces.

The Body's Role

One thing you can't escape is the role of the musculature in your hands, arms, and fingers. If you learn to work with your body, not against it, you can make the most of your ability. Just as you do for any other physical activity, you should warm up every time you play. Warming up can be a simple scale exercise or a daily practice routine.

Carpal Tunnel Syndrome and Tendonitis

If you overuse or misuse your wrists, you risk developing either carpal tunnel syndrome or tendonitis, or both, which can bring your guitar career to a fast end. Tendon swelling can be aggravated by repetitive or strenuous activities, and some people experience repetitive stress injuries if they perform the same motion over and over again. More than one well-known player has been affected by these, but professionals don't usually like to talk about it.

ALERT!

If you ever have any pain from playing guitar, stop playing and rest your hands for the rest of the day. If the problem persists, seek medical advice.

The Bent Fist

Let's prove, in a very dramatic fashion, that a bent wrist causes stress. Lay your arm, palm up on a table. Make sure your wrist is flat, and try to make a fist. Nothing hard or uncomfortable about that motion is there? Now bend your hand toward your wrist and try to make a fist with your wrist bent. Do you feel the tremendous strain in the back of your wrist? That's because your tendons are being stretched and not being allowed to work properly. Most players play with a bent wrist, but because they never force their hand into a fist, they never realize how much strain they're putting on the tendons. But, in reality, the tendons in the hand are getting stretched the exact same way as they are when you tried this experiment; you just don't feel it.

What Do I Do?

Playing correctly is not just better for your body, it actually makes playing easier. If certain chords hurt you before, especially barre chords, learning how to use your hands effectively will change the way you play.

To Sit or Stand?

A hand problem usually gets worse when you stand up to play, because you assume a poor standing position. It seems to be cool these days to play your guitar slung way down low. Having the guitar down that low forces you to play with a bent wrist just to reach the guitar! The guitar should be at the same place on your body whether you sit or stand. Usually if your guitar rests against your stomach area, you're in the right area. When you're wearing a strap, the guitar should not move when you stand up or sit down. Keeping the guitar a little higher on your body allows your hands to work properly. If it looks a little "uncool" to you, just imagine pain in your wrists that never goes away. You can learn to live with the guitar up high, but do you want to learn to live with the pain?

Maintaining good posture when you practice is very important; try to sit in a comfortable chair. And if you read music from a stand, keep the music at eye level so you don't strain your neck.

Take Advantage of the Mirror

Every so often, play in front of a mirror. Really look at your hands, and see what your posture looks like. Look at side angles so you can see the slope of your fretting hand (normally hidden by your guitar neck). The ideal position is to have totally straight wrists on both hands. Although this isn't always 100 percent possible, especially when playing on the lower strings, just try to have as little bend as possible in your wrists.

If you find that you have the tendency to bend your wrists, play in front of a mirror every day and scrutinize yourself. Be diligent about this, because you can retrain your hands to do the right things. Many students find that after they fix wrist problems they have more speed than they had before. Excess tension can rob you of precious energy that you could be directing elsewhere—speed.

The Fingers' Effort

Humans weren't designed to use fingers for strength-related exercises. Our fingers also weren't expected to work individually; they usually work as a group. This is why when you bend one finger, the others bend a little, too. The reality is that your fingers individually aren't very strong and don't have a lot of power. Their muscles are relatively small and are much weaker than those in other parts of your body.

Your thumb is a hard finger to deal with. It's typically not used on your fretting hand, and because of this, it tends to sit in one spot behind the neck of the guitar. The location of the thumb can greatly contribute to problems with your technique and wrist placement. If your thumb is too high on the neck so that you can see it sticking out, your hands will have a hard time reaching chords. If your thumb is too low, you'll have to bend your wrist to reach the low notes. The best place for your thumb is dead in the middle of the neck—not too high and not too low.

How hard do you have to press a note down on the fret board? As little as possible. Let's do an experiment. Try fretting a note on the guitar (pressing down on the fret and picking a string)—any note you want. To start with, fret the note too lightly, and you should hear a slight thud. Now gradually increase the pressure slightly until you hear a buzz. Then finally press harder to hear the note come out. That's exactly how hard you should hit the note, and for players who are used to pressing down quite hard, this may be a revelation to you. It takes just a little bit of force to make a note sound. If you're able to play softer and lighter, you'll have more energy left for other things. If you're into playing fast, this is the first step to reaching your goal. No one plays fast and pushes down hard on notes; actually it's the speed demons who make it look like their hands are just gliding along effortlessly.

The Art of Playing

Enough anatomy; let's talk about technique as it directly relates to guitar playing. You shouldn't try to develop your right and left hands separately, especially if you want to play fast. Your hands need to work together, not apart. They are discussed separately here because each hand does a different job.

The Picking Hand

Your picking hand has the noble job of starting the note—of giving it life, so to speak. Essentially, the pick moves in a back and forth motion through the string. The most efficient way to pick is to alternate strokes up and down. When you want to play fast, alternate-picking is a must, but rhythm playing is sometimes more comfortable with all down strokes. It's safe to say that lead playing is almost exclusively alternate-picked. Traditionally, guitar players use small plastic picks, or plectrums, to strike the string for a clear sound. Billy Gibbons, from ZZ Top, uses a U.S. quarter to pick, and some players play entirely with only their fingers.

Finger style is beyond the scope of our discussions. There are so many different ways to hold the pick and so many different motions used to move it back and forth that you could go crazy trying to figure out the best way to do it. Choose a way and stick with it. Unless you need to fix an improper hand position, changing your picking position can stunt your development. Whatever you chose, develop it to its fullest. There have been great players who held the pick in the strangest ways, yet it works for them. Who are we to argue?

ALERT!

You should never practice your picking hand separately from your fretting hand. The art of playing is to synchronize the two hands to play together. Overdeveloping one aspect of your playing can hurt your overall growth.

The Fretting Hand

To press a string down with the least amount of force, your finger has to be very close to the fret. The farther it is from the fret, the harder it is to play that note. As you get closer to the fret, the amount of force necessary goes down. Once you get used to playing next to the fret, it isn't very hard to do it all the time. On the higher frets, it's hard not to play close to the fret because they're so close together. The tip of the finger, not the flat part, should hit the string. Your finger should form a smooth curve and should not collapse. **FIGURE 11-1** shows what your hand

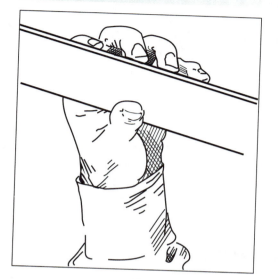

FIGURE 11-1 Proper hand position

should look like when you're fretting. Notice how each finger is on its tip and is curved. This is what it should look like; no strain or force is necessary to achieve this.

The great martial arts personality Bruce Lee demonstrated a startling technique called the two-inch punch. Lee could place his fist two inches away from some poor volunteer's chest and with no windup, blast the victim across the room. He was able to focus all his energy into a small movement. You can do the same thing with your fingers; they don't require an extensive windup to work. The amount of space your fingers travel when striking a note directly affects your speed. If your fingers have to travel from far away to reach a note you'll have a hard time playing fast. Keep your fingers close to the fingerboard when they're not in use. The closer they are, the faster they can strike the note. How do you get your fingers closer? Simply relax them when you aren't using them.

Building Good Technique

You may wonder how other players get such great chops. Was it practice, natural ability, or just plain luck? First, you don't get anything for free. No one starts playing guitar with instant speed—everyone has to work at it. Technique is a mental mindset more than physical ability. You will play as fast as you want to play. If you've spent your whole life emulating fast players, then you'll have a yearning to play fast. If you play slow-hand blues and are content to take it easy, good technique can be as simple as learning to use your hands efficiently.

These are a few things you need to help you develop good technique:

- A metronome
- A logbook

- A pencil
- A goal

A metronome is an indispensable tool for working on technique, because it gives you a means of measuring your progress. Rather than just "feeling" fast today, wouldn't it be nice to know that you could play exactly ten beats per minute faster? The pencil and logbook will enable you to chart your development. Setting a realistic goal—mastering some licks or solos that are too hard for you right now—gives you something to work toward, and you'll feel great after you achieve that goal.

Building speed is a long process that requires a lot of determination and hard work. Practice every day and chart your growth with a metronome.

Exercises to Improve Technique

Trying to prescribe general technical exercises can be very difficult. Every type of playing has its own peculiarities; it's hard to prepare for everything that may come your way. The best exercises to start with are simple ones that help your hands learn to work as a team. Exercises that utilize every finger and a pick stroke for every finger are beneficial. **FIGURE 11-2** is a great example to play every day—a simple chromatic scale warmup played in the fifth position.

This exercise contains a few important technical elements. First, it exercises each of your four fingers. It is also an easy pattern to work with. Chromatic patterns are great for working on relaxing your hands because the patterns are so easy to remember that they let you focus your energy on other things. For the picking hand, this provides you with four picks per string without a whole lot of jumping around. Many great players do this warmup every day.

Use the metronome to chart your progress. Start at a slow speed; say 60 beats per minute, and play four notes per click (one click on each string). As you start to feel more comfortable, gradually increase the speed by five beats per minute (65, 70, and so on). In a few short months you'll be playing better and faster.

FIGURE 11-2 Chromatic warmup

TRACK 48

The truth is that anything can be a good technique exercise. A simple scale practiced every day with a metronome can build speed. Anything can work for this as long as you use the metronome to increase the difficulty. What you should practice are the things that are hard for you. Each player is different; we all find certain things hard and other things easy. Focus on things that are hard for you.

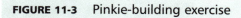

FIGURE 11-3 Pinkie-building exercise

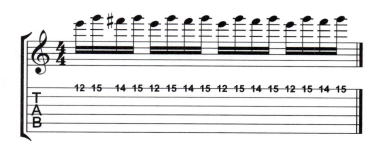

There are a few spots that everyone finds difficult. For most players, using their third and fourth fingers on their fretting hand is a real challenge. Many players avoid the pinkie altogether and stretch everything with their third finger. **FIGURE 11-3** shows a great exercise to overcome that problem.

FIGURE 11-4 String-skipping practice

Another common problem is string skipping with the picking hand. Landing accurately without looking down can be a real challenge. **FIGURE 11-4** is a nice exercise using an A-Major barre chord to practice string skipping.

Remember, learning good technique is important. You were given only one set of hands and muscles—treat them right. Learning to relax when you play is one of the hardest aspects of playing well, and it is the most important part—one that doesn't get as much attention as it should. Start early, and get it right.

Chapter 12

Extended Techniques: Tapping and Sweeping

Getting beyond the basic world of the alternate-picking technique can yield some exciting results. Modern guitar playing has championed some extended techniques that allow the guitar to create unique sounds. "Extended technique" refers to a way of playing that goes beyond the normal and accepted way. Among these techniques are tapping and sweep-picking. This chapter shows you how to apply these techniques to your own playing.

Stretching the Boundaries

Standard playing, which uses a pick in one hand and four fingers on the other, is not the only way to play a guitar. Over the years, players have stretched the boundaries by exploring extended techniques. One of the best places to start is with two-handed tapping, a technique made popular by Eddie Van Halen.

In 1978, the world as guitar players knew it was changed. On the first Van Halen album, a long unaccompanied guitar solo performed by guitarist Eddie Van Halen utilized two-handed tapping. The piece entitled "Eruption" is a milestone for guitar playing and has expanded the repertoire of technique for guitar players everywhere. While Eddie wasn't the first to tap, he was the first to successfully integrate it into his playing. Tapping had been used in classical guitar playing, and other rock players had tried to integrate it into their playing, but Eddie took it and made it his own in a way the others had not.

While Eddie Van Halen may have started the ball rolling, other players have taken tapping to new heights. Stanley Jordan is one of the most amazing two-hand tapping players out there, and his solo version of "Stairway to Heaven" is incredible. Many modern rock players have adopted tapping as part of their normal technique: Steve Vai, Joe Satriani, Kirk Hammett, Diamond Darrell, John Petrucci, and others continue to evolve tapping in the rock context.

Tap Mechanics

Tapping involves placing both hands on the fingerboard. For those whose picking hand has been exiled to strumming, this will be new for you. On an electric guitar the amplifier makes it possible to play very lightly and have the notes heard clearly, something that is impossible on an acoustic guitar. On the electric guitar, you can use the four fingers on your picking hand to play notes on the fingerboard. The amplifier eliminates the need for picking and frees the other hand to join in the fun. Tapping enables you to play things that just aren't possible with a pick technique. Your two

FIGURE 12-1   Pre-tap hammer-ons

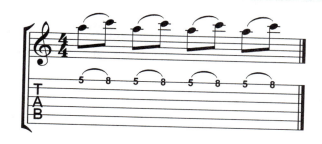

TRACK 49

FIGURE 12-2   Tapping example

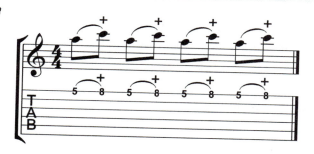

hands can be separated at either extreme of the neck and you can play rapid-fire licks that sound as though you've jumped up and down the neck rapidly, even though you haven't moved at all.

Let's begin with a very simple example of a tap. **FIGURE 12-1** doesn't involve tapping at all; it's just a hammer-on between the first finger and the pinkie, and gets you ready for the tap.

Now replace the pinkie with a tapped finger from your picking hand (right hand for right-handed player, left for left-handed). Most players tap with their index finger, although the middle also works well. Experiment to see what works best for you. Some players tap with their middle finger so that they don't have to drop their pick while tapping. If you opt for the index finger, you'll have to switch the pick to another finger while you tap.

In **FIGURE 12-2**, you replace the pinkie with whichever tapping finger you choose. Reach up with your picking hand, place it alongside your other hand, and use a finger from your picking hand to replace the pinkie.

In the music, the notes that are tapped are marked with a + sign, so you can easily see what to tap. Treat the tap as you do any other hammer-on—hammer down hard to make the note sound right. If you've never tapped, it may take you a while to get used to using your fingers this way and to get used to the new sensation in your picking-hand fingertips.

Tap Pull-Offs

You can also pull-off with your tapped finger to keep the string "alive." This is especially useful when you loop a small lick over and over again. To pull-off, after you finish the tap, pull away from the string with a slight downward motion just as you did with a normal fret-board pull-off. Pull-offs help articulate the note and make it sound clearer; they also give the next note on the lick (usually a normally fretted note) some volume. If you just let your finger leave the string, there's no energy to make the next note sound, and since you're tapping, you really can't pick in between. Pull-offs are vital to tapping. The harder you pull-off, the more accent you give the next note.

Tap Benefits

Tapping gives you certain advantages that you can't accomplish any other way. In **FIGURE 12-2**, you went back and forth between the first finger and the pinkie. Normally, the pinkie is a weak finger and unless

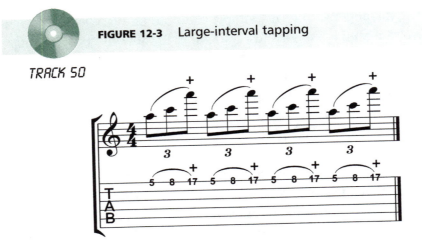

FIGURE 12-3   Large-interval tapping

TRACK 50

you've spent a lot of time developing its muscles, you won't be able to hammer-on very fast or hard. By replacing the weak pinkie with a strong index finger from the other hand, you can achieve greater speed and flexibility. Tapping also gives you the ability to play wide intervals smoothly. When you jump around the neck, it can be a real challenge to connect the notes smoothly, especially when shifting. But by using two hands, you can reach notes that are far apart, like the ones in **FIGURE 12-3**. This line would be very difficult to play if it weren't tapped.

Another great perk with tapping is that you gain extra fingers. You're no longer limited to four fingers; you can easily add a fifth or more. Guitarist Stanley Jordan is one of the first to take tapping and apply it to chordal playing. He uses all eight fingers to tap with, which sounds as though several guitarists are playing at once.

Tapping Scales

Let's apply tapping to a major scale. Use the tapping finger to extend your reach so that you don't have to shift at the top of the scale. The lick in the next figure uses a tap at the top of the scale, so you will have to pick until that point. When it comes time to tap, glide your picking hand to the fingerboard, tap, and return to pick the rest of the scale. This is called hybrid tapping and is an easy way to integrate tapping into your everyday playing. Hybrid tapping gives you the best of both worlds—tapping and picking. See **FIGURE 12-4**.

FIGURE 12-4   G-Major scale extended with tapping

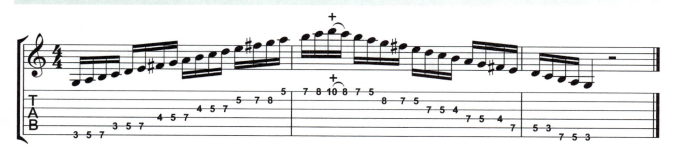

FIGURE 12-5 Extended scale example using taps

TRACK 51

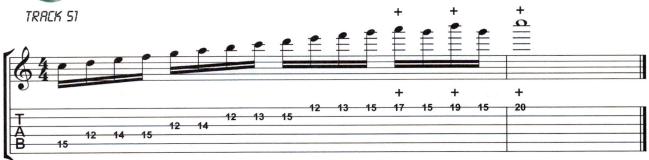

Tapping can be a nice addition to your normal technique. **FIGURE 12-5** is a more complicated example that uses the tap to embellish the end of a major-scale lick. The taps are used to extend the scale up beyond its normal reach.

Use your imagination to see where tapping can fit into scales. You've only scratched the surface of tapping scales here.

Tapping Chords

As chordal players, guitarists are limited by the nature of the guitar. Four fingers and six strings don't always produce the results you hear in your head. However, if you use your other four fingers to add to your chords, the possibilities multiply, because taps extend the range of the chords. **FIGURE 12-6** shows an example of a C-Major chord played as a barre chord, with a tap added higher on the neck to extend the chord.

Joe Satriani's tune "Midnight" is an amazing example of two-handed chords—without the tapping, the piece would be unplayable. Chordal tapping is less common in rock and blues music. Besides Stanley Jordan, who is the king of chordal tapping, the

FIGURE 12-6
C-Major
chord with
extension
tap

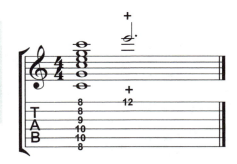

field is wide open. If you're looking for a unique slant on playing guitar, playing two hands all the time may be just right for you.

FACT

There is an instrument called The Stick that's designed specifically for tapping. It comes in various models, but all have more than the standard six strings. If you like to tap, you'll love The Stick.

Arpeggio Tapping

One of the reasons that "Eruption" was so successful is the material that Van Halen chose to tap. The tapping segment of "Eruption" is based on arpeggios played across a single string. Since he didn't have to change strings, the flow of the notes sounds uninterrupted. Let's apply this concept to some simple arpeggios across the E string. For example, you can take an A-minor arpeggio (A, C, E) and turn it into a tapping arpeggio. You can easily play the A and the C with the first and fourth fingers on the fifth and eighth frets respectively; and you can play the E with a tap. Put these together, and you get the arpeggio tapping in **FIGURE 12-7**.

To make this lick really work well you need to repeat it in a looping fashion. Repeating the same small shapes several times is what made "Eruption" work so well. You can use this method for any arpeggio you think of—diminished, major, and minor all work well. If you want to be

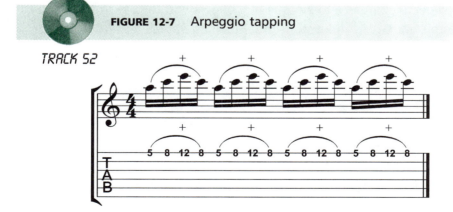

FIGURE 12-7 Arpeggio tapping

TRACK 52

FIGURE 12-8 E-diminished arpeggio tapped

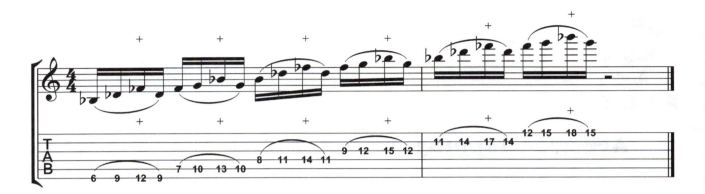

really adventurous, you can use more fingers to tap. You can even add more notes from the chord!

FIGURE 12-8 is an example showing an E-diminished seventh arpeggio with tapping. This long example is worth the effort.

Like any other technique, tapping is just another tool to get the job done. When you apply it to musical situations, you can have great success; but don't just tap for the sake of tapping. Tapping is most effective in situations where tapping lets you play licks you can't do any other way.

The Mechanics of Sweep-Picking

Sweep-picking is a technique that allows you to play arpeggios at a very rapid rate. As you know, normal picking entails up and down, or alternate, picking. You also know that, normally, arpeggios contain only one note per string, and move up and down the fret board very quickly. If you ever tried it, you know that trying to alternate-pick only one note per string is a real challenge. Some very smart guitar player looked at the problem and said, "Why can't I just pick it all in one direction?" Instead of alternating your pick strokes up and down, let your pick glide, or "sweep," in one direction using gravity to move your pick through the strings.

This is a much more efficient way to pick arpeggios, and as a result you can really hit the gas pedal with this technique. But it's not just for fast players; the technique is so efficient that you may find yourself doing it on examples other than arpeggios. This technique may have stemmed from a violin technique. Violinists drag their bow in fast passages because it's inefficient to bow up and down.

There are more sloppy sweep-pickers in the world than you can imagine, and this is because there's a shortage of solid instruction on how to sweep beyond just "gliding the pick." Four main factors go into sweep-picking:

- Synchronization
- Separation

- Muting
- String-catching

Sweep-Picking in Practice

Synchronizing your hands is hard, no matter how you intend to play. Sweep-picking demands synchronization, because it moves so quickly. To work on getting the two hands to play well together, you need to eliminate some difficulty for your fretting hand and focus just on the picking part. For this, you use shapes that do not make real chords, as shown in **FIGURE 12-9**. Actually, the shapes sound pretty strange; however, they do serve a good purpose: they let you focus on your picking hand.

FIGURE 12-9   Sweep-picking practice pattern

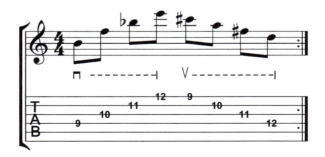

Sweep-picking isn't like playing a chord and strumming though the notes fast. On the fret board, only one finger needs to play at a time, and this is where separation comes in. Essentially, you let your fingers roll from string to string, otherwise the notes bleed together like a chord, which you don't want. When you do this correctly only one finger is down at a time, and that finger should coincide with the pick stroke.

Both hands play a part in the muting process. (Muting can be used quite often, not just in sweeping.) To keep the other strings quiet when you're not playing them, use the fleshy part of your palm to mute the strings you're not playing. Proper muting is essential to playing with distortion and absolutely critical when playing with a lot of distortion. Your fret-board fingers can also lightly mute strings that aren't in play. Muting is a subtle technique that you refine all your life, so keep trying to quiet those unruly lower strings that tend to ring out when they're not supposed to. This will clean up your playing greatly.

One of the world's great sweep-pickers is Frank Gambale. Gambale can sweep just about anything, and his command of the technique will amaze you. Other notable sweep-pickers are Yngwie Malmsteen, John Petrucci, Steve Vai, Jason Becker, and Marty Friedman.

String-catching is letting the next string catch your pick after you move through the string before it. This also aids in the separation of the notes. When you sweep, put a bit of force into the string so you get a nice positive attack on the note. This hard click may sound bad when slow, but at high speeds it helps define the notes very clearly.

Practicing sweeping is unlike any other technique on guitar; it's much harder to play slow than it is to play fast. When sweeping is done correctly, it's an incredibly efficient and graceful motion. When you practice it slowly, it's hard to get a sense of the fluid motion, but keep at it anyway. While it may be difficult to practice sweeping, it really is the only way to truly become a great sweeper.

Real Sweeping

For an arpeggio shape to work well, it should have only one note per string. There are some exceptions to this, but for now you'll work on some simple shapes that contain only one note per string.

For major arpeggios, the shapes with roots on the fifth string work well for this purpose. The B-Major arpeggio example in **FIGURE 12-10** will get you started. Notice on the musical notation where the pick turns around at the top of the lick. The down picks look like a staple, while the up picks resemble a V.

To make the previous example minor, lower the third (D♯) to D, and you come up with **FIGURE 12-11**.

FIGURE 12-10   B-Major arpeggio swept

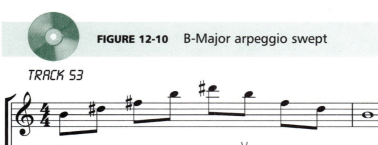

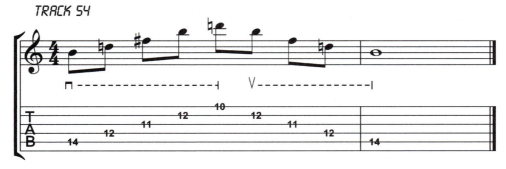

FIGURE 12-11   B-minor arpeggio swept

To extend the range of licks you can sweep, you need to add more than one note to a string. This is done with a hammer-on. Look at the example in **FIGURE 12-12** of an A-minor arpeggio.

Notice that you added a hammer-on to the fifth and first string. This causes a slight delay in the picking motion. You don't exactly have one

FIGURE 12-12   A-minor arpeggio with hammer-ons

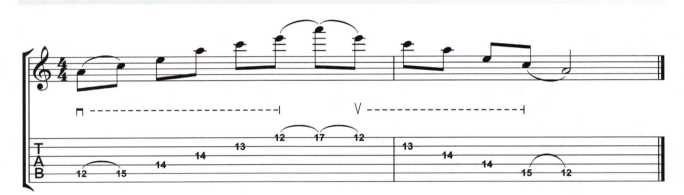

FIGURE 12-13   C-minor arpeggio swept with tap

TRACK 55

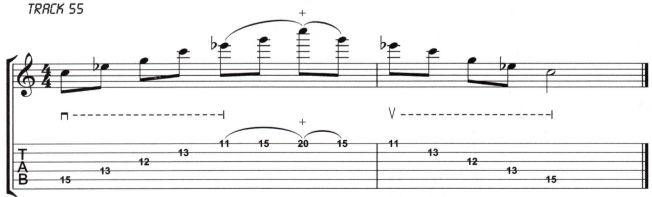

finger to a pick stroke anymore. You have to wait for the hammer-on to complete before you pick. Thankfully, the hammer-ons occur quickly, and it doesn't take much to get used to the slight delay.

You can apply sweeping to any of the arpeggios in Chapter 9. You can even create your own. Sweeping doesn't have to be limited to just arpeggios, you can sweep any notes that fall on consecutive strings.

Want to try combining these new extended techniques? For **FIGURE 12-13** you'll use a C-minor arpeggio with a hammer-on at the top of the lick, and a tap to extend the lick even further. This lick is definitely not for the faint of heart, but if you're up for a challenge you'll find it here.

The really tricky part of this lick is the tap; the sweep by itself doesn't present any real problems. The tap requires that, after you get to the top of the lick, you move your picking hand to the neck, tap quickly, and then return to pick the rest of the sweep. It's a difficult move, but if you practice this slowly enough, you can master it and impress your friends.

Chapter 13

Guitar Tricks

Guitar players have invented many clever ways to play the instrument to take advantage of its unique characteristics. Some tricks are merely modifications of your current technique, while others involve gadgets. This chapter explores the unique ways to play the guitar, and the fun noises and sounds you can create with it.

Pick a Spot

Everyone looks for ways to change their tone. Whether they're trying to emulate the sound of a great player or they're looking for new sounds, most players look to different guitars and amps for tone changes. In reality, guitars and amps have little to do with your tone; it originates from your hands.

Have you ever noticed that, while Eddie Van Halen has changed guitars and amps over the course of his life, he still sounds the same? Although string gauge, string height, and pick can make some difference, the sound of his guitar has more to do with the way he approaches the instrument than the equipment he uses.

The most immediate tone change you can get comes from moving the location of your pick. The guitar, especially the acoustic guitar, has a remarkable range of colors that you can create just by changing where you pick. Most players tend to pick halfway between the end of the neck and the bridge. This is a nice place to pick because it gives you an excellent round sound for most playing situations. But move away from this central spot and you alter your tone dramatically.

Experiment with pick placement for some dramatic tone changes. If you pick closer to the bridge, you'll get a more metallic sound; as you approach the fingerboard, you'll get a very sweet, syrupy sound. Playing closer to the neck can help an appealing chordal passage sound more delicate. Playing up near the bridge can help to emphasize a lead part or an important melody that needs to stand out.

FACT

On an electric guitar, you'll get some changes in tone by changing where you pick, but the effect will be much more pronounced on an acoustic guitar.

Controlling Sounds on an Electric Guitar

Are you puzzled by all of the control knobs and switches on your electric guitar? Many guitar students, especially beginners, have little idea what the controls on an electric guitar do. Most electric guitars have three main control knobs—the volume knob(s), tone knob(s), and the pickup selector, which is what transfers the sound of the guitar to the amplifier.

Volume

Volume knobs may seem fairly self-explanatory, but there are some things you may not know about them. When your guitar is going through a clean amplifier with no distortion, a volume knob acts just as you think it should: It controls the volume of the instrument. However, when you apply distortion to your sound you'll notice that the volume knob no longer controls the overall volume. When distortion is turned on, the volume knob acts as a distortion filter, essentially turning up and down the level of distortion. You can change your guitar from a semiclean sound by turning the volume knob down (but not off) while distortion is on. As you turn the volume knob up, your guitar sound becomes more distorted. This is a handy way to make adjustments without bending down to change your effect pedal, or amp distortion settings mid-song.

Tone

The tone knob adjusts the frequencies that go through the guitar and into the amplifier. By changing the position of the tone knob, you can adjust the sound from treble to bass (just as you do with the tone knob on stereo equipment). When the tone knob is all the way up (10), the guitar acts normally—the tone knob is not doing anything but letting the natural sound of the pickups pass through to the speakers. Rolling the knob down limits the amount of high frequencies the guitar emits, so the sound gets muddier and more bass heavy. This has long been a secret of jazz and blues players who want to warm up their clean sound. The tone knob can dramatically alter your sound, so experiment with it!

Pickup Selector

Pickup switches typically come in two varieties: Stratocaster 5 position and Les Paul 3 position. Each serves the same purpose. Did you ever wonder why you have pickups at different spots on the guitar? The location of the pickup affects the sound, just as the location of the pick affects the sound on an acoustic guitar.

The pickup closer to the bridge has a more treble-like sound; the pickup closer to the neck sounds sweeter and has more bass. The pickup selector chooses between the different pickup locations and thus acts as the sound selector—when the pickup selector is in the forward position (toward the neck) the sound is softer; when the pickup selector is in the back position (the bridge) the sound is heavier.

Traditionally, the neck pickup is used for solos and clean chords, and the bridge pickup is used for distorted chords and heavier rhythmic parts. For guitars with three pickups, the middle position gives you a nice in-between sound.

Add-Ons

Now we get to the fun stuff. There are things that you can add to the guitar to change the sound. The place to start is the last place you might think to look: the pick. The pick is the direct connection between you and the guitar and has the greatest effect on your tone. Many players just pick with whatever is convenient, while others realize that variety is the spice of life (and sound).

The Twenty-Five-Cent Tone Shift

The number of picks on the market is staggering. The variety of different materials, colors, shapes, and thicknesses make for much variation. Some players are content to stick with the normal Fender-type heavy pick, while others prefer small teardrop-shaped picks. If you've been using the same pick for a long time, buy some new picks. Most picks are about twenty-five cents each, so buy several. Experiment with shape, hardness, and material—each pick will give you a different sound. You can even buy picks made out of steel and copper (heavy metal?). You may be shocked at how much a new pick can affect your sound.

Certain picks are better suited to certain types of playing. Rhythm players tend to like light picks that have a fair amount of flex. The flex helps facilitate strumming without getting in the way. Players who enjoy playing fast tend to like small, hard picks. The size lets them move around the guitar with more efficiency, and the hardness translates directly to speed: the harder the pick, the faster it moves through the strings.

FACT

Don't think that you have to hold the pick point down all the time. Try turning your pick every which way for different sounds, especially upside down. You don't even have to use a pick at all. Many players successfully use their fingers to play. Mark Knopfler of Dire Straits uses his fingers all the time. Some acoustic players grow out their fingernails to imitate the sounds of a pick, while others use the fleshy pads of their fingers.

Strings

Strings are another crucial factor that influences your sound. The type of metal they're made of and the gauge of string can change your sound dramatically. Bigger is better. The heavier gauge you can use, the better and fatter your tone will be. Light strings can sound anemic and weak. If you play on 9-gauge strings, try going to 10, and you'll notice a nice change, especially in the low end. Stevie Ray Vaughan is legendary for using 13-gauge strings on his guitar. These huge strings contributed to his huge tone.

If you play acoustic guitar, experiment with gauge and metal types. You can commonly find strings of bronze, phosphor bronze, and other metals. These different metal wraps have an effect on your sound. For you speed freaks, lighter is better (usually). Many shredders like Yngwie Malmsteen use 8-gauge strings because the lightened string gauge helps increase overall facility. Heavy strings can make bending very difficult, so if you plan to increase your string gauge, do it slowly in steps so you can get used to the new tension.

Every time you change your string gauge, you should have your guitar set up by a qualified repairman. The new string tension may affect the neck angle and intonation.

Capos

A capo is a small device that attaches to the neck of the guitar. It changes the location of the nut so that the open position can be replicated in other places on the neck. Usually, capos are an elastic wraparound or spring-loaded clamp. The spring-loaded clamp is often easier to take off and on. Capos can cost between $10 and $15.

In first position, you get certain chords that are easy to play. For the most part, the pitches of the open strings dictate these chords. Because these chords contain open strings, they're easier to play than barre chords. A capo allows you to play the easy shapes from the first position, yet have different chords come out. It's very useful for transposing chords to other keys. For instance, many singers/songwriters use capos to match the natural keys of their voice while keeping the chord shapes simple. Try placing a capo across the third fret. No matter what capo you use, it's important to get the capo right next to the third fret, but not on it! Once you're set, go ahead and play what you know as an open C chord. With the capo, all your open strings are three frets higher so you're not playing the C chord anymore. You're playing the C chord shape, but it is now a E♭ because the capo has changed the open strings. Before, the E♭ chord involved an uncomfortable barre. Now, with a capo on the third fret . . .

- C becomes E♭.
- G becomes B♭.
- A becomes C.
- D becomes F.

FACT

Capos are usually used in acoustic playing, especially southern rock and country styles. The Eagles used a capo on the intro to "Hotel California."

The capo can be placed anywhere on the neck you want. The third fret is a handy spot because it gives you chords that are very difficult to achieve in the first position. Using the capo effectively will allow you to play parts that are otherwise impossible.

If you play a song with a lot of barre chords, the capo makes your life easier. Try it on different frets to see how the simple chord shapes change.

Physics 101 and Natural Harmonics

Harmonics are the tones made by vibrating strings to produce overtones. When you pluck a string, the string vibrates in waves. However, there are points along the string where there is no motion; this point is called a node. (If you remember a sine wave from math class, it crosses the zero point, and that's called a node.) A guitar string has many nodes, which always cut the string in half. For an open string, cutting the string into two equal parts takes you to the twelfth fret, which is the first node.

So what does this have to do with harmonics? At these node points, you can play a harmonic. Harmonics are played with a very different technique than other notes on the guitar. To play a harmonic, you don't push the string down; instead you lightly place your finger directly over the twelfth fret and just barely touch it. As long as you're directly over the twelfth fret, and you haven't pushed down too hard, you will get a note. This note is the same note that you would have gotten had you played the twelfth fret normally. But because the note is a harmonic, it has a unique sound.

If you want to play harmonics, go to the pickup closest to the bridge. If you're on an acoustic guitar, pick closer to the bridge. Playing in that area will help the harmonics ring out clearly. Distortion will also help.

One of the neat things about harmonics is that after you play the harmonic, the string will continue to ring out; you don't have to leave your finger over the twelfth fret. Leaving your finger over the fret may mute the note, so after you play it, get out of the way and let it ring. Harmonics like this exist all over the guitar because you can keep dividing the string in half forever! The most popular harmonics are the twelfth fret, the seventh fret, and the fifth fret. Playing harmonics from open strings is called natural harmonics. They occur on every string and on almost every fret. Some frets have harmonics that are so high that you can barely hear them—that's why they don't always sound great.

Artificial Harmonics

Artificial harmonics are those amazing-sounding notes that seem to scream out from a lead guitar solo. Artificial harmonics are relatively easy to play, but are very hard to explain. You may get a little frustrated while trying to get these to work. Keep trying and you will be able to do it in no time!

Artificial harmonics have little to do with natural harmonics. While they're both called harmonics and both use nodes of a vibrating string, the technique behind them is quite different. Artificial harmonics are done from your picking hand; your fretting hand plays normally as it always does. Now, here's the hard part—to play an artificial harmonic you need to choke up on the pick and let only a bit of it show. There should be only a nub sticking out. When you go to pick a note, instead of picking and then getting out of the way as you normally do, pick with a slight downward angle, forcing a small part of your thumb to hit the string. If you choked up enough, the fat part of your thumb should be right there. You'll need to do a lot of experimenting to find the sweet spot!

ALERT!

It's easy to get caught up in shapes when you play because guitar is such a visually oriented instrument. Every once in a while, try turning out the lights and playing guitar in the dark. By removing the visual aspect of playing, you will force your ear to take over. Your ear may lead you to some places you never imagined—or heard!

There are several sweet spots, and most exist right over the sound hole, or between the pickups. Since you are very high up on the string, you get a very high harmonic. But there's a catch: The location of the harmonics changes every time you fret a different note. So don't think that because you've found the location for one note it will work for every note. The good news is that the nodes are very close together, so you're bound to hit one of them. The secret to this technique is getting your thumb to hit the string at the same time that the pick does. If you're early or late, you'll hear a thud. If you hit it right, you'll get a high note that seems to come from nowhere.

Harmonics like this require some form of distortion to come out well. You can play them clean, but they sound much better with distortion on. Until you get the feel of this, you may be frustrated, but keep trying. Artificial harmonics are a staple of rock guitar playing. Once you figure out the technique, you never forget it.

The EBow

The EBow is a small hand-held device that uses a magnetic force field to make a guitar string vibrate forever (or until the battery runs out). Unfortunately acoustic players are left out of this party, because it works only in combination with a magnetic pickup and an amplifier. It sets up a loop between the pickup and the string, causing the string to vibrate seemingly forever. Because you use the EBow in lieu of a pick, there's no pick attack, and the sound is very smooth. The EBow can generate some wild effects on the guitar, and in the right hands, can be a wonderfully creative tool.

Many players have used the EBow on recordings. The performance that stands out is REM's Peter Buck and his EBow playing on "What's the Frequency, Kenneth?" John Petrucci of Dream Theater also uses an EBow on the album *Six Degrees of Inner Turbulence,* and Metallica uses one on "Unforgiven." You will find the EBow listed in everyone's trick bag and gear list. It's relatively inexpensive (between $80 and $100) and can lead to some very original results.

Slides

A slide is a finger device that temporarily takes the place of a fret; unlike a fret, a slide can be moved around freely. The use of slides could take the rest of this book to discuss completely, but this section will at least get you started. Playing with slides began with the blues. Early slides were bottle necks from beer bottles and small medicine bottles. Modern slides are made of glass or metal and are molded to perfectly match your finger; they come in different shapes and sizes to match every player. They run from around $5 to $10.

Slide Mechanics

Because slides can move around "in between" the frets, they're great for imitating the voice, which naturally scoops and slides between the notes. The slide rests gently on top of the string, and like a harmonic, doesn't push down, but floats along the length of the string.

When playing slides, you have to determine what finger you want to place the slide on—middle, ring, or pinky finger. Most players use their middle or ring finger. You can't use the index finger because an essential part of slide playing is muting behind the slide to keep the strings quiet. If you put the slide on your index finger, you won't have a finger to mute with. Pick the finger that can reach all the strings comfortably.

In Tune

Playing a slide can be great fun, but if it's not played in tune, no one will want to hear it. The fret takes care of the tuning for you, but when you play with a slide, the slide takes over for the fret. You have to control where the slide is on the string in order to tune the note. To get the slide in tune, you must be directly over the fret. Because this can be difficult, many slide players use back and forth vibrato motion to hide their tuning problems—which is fine and sounds vocal-like (shhh . . . that's why singers use vibrato, too).

Application

The slide mimics your fretting hand, so you can use it on scales, single notes, and some chords, but because the slide is a straight line, it works only on a few chords. The slide is used for the blues scale almost exclusively. You can trace the scale shape with the slide in the same way that you play it with your fingers. Because the slide is straight across, you can jump to adjacent frets much easier than normal. When you use a slide, try to use it differently. Don't just recreate your old licks with a slide—try to create new ones that are not possible without the slide.

Alternate Tuning

Alternate tuning implies that you are retuning the strings to anything other than standard E-A-D-G-B-E tuning. Alternate tunings are great for

FIGURE 13-1   Power chords in drop-D tuning

finding new chord shapes and unusual sounds that aren't possible on a standard tuned guitar. You will need a good chromatic tuner to help retune your strings. Here are three examples of some common alternate tunings:

- Drop-D tuning: Drop your lowest E string down one whole step to D. The strings are then D, A, D, G, B, E. Drop D is useful for heavy music because it gives you some lower power chords. Power chords can be played with one finger. Look at **FIGURE 13-1**.
- "DADGAD" tuning: Tune your sixth string down to D, second string down to A, and first string down to D. Leave the others unchanged. This is a common tuning that can give you some unexpected results. Jimmy Page used this on "Black Mountain Side."
- Open-E tuning: Tune the fifth string up to B, fourth string up to E, and third string up to G♯. Leave the others unchanged. Open-E tuning is a great slide tuning because you can play major chords with a straight slide played across one fret. It's also a nice tuning because your open strings make a nice-sounding E chord.

There are millions of other tunings, and you should try to invent new ones. Typically, alternate tunings are great for one song here and there, not for exclusive use. (But don't tell that to Joni Mitchell, who plays exclusively in open alternate tunings.) Ⓔ

Chapter 14

Putting It All Together: Blues

The information in the previous chapters gives you a solid basis on how music and theory apply to guitar playing. Now you're ready to apply these concepts to building licks and constructing musical phrases. This chapter shows you what can be done when you apply scales, chords, and theory to the blues progression.

Blues Solo Riffs in A

The first line in the example in **FIGURE 14-1** is a derivation of a simple minor pentatonic scale in the key of A. What makes this lick different is the addition of the C♯, which is the major third of A. Even though blues is predominantly played in a minor scale, most of the chords are major. Adding the C♯ helps to better conform the scale to the chord. You'll find licks that sound like this in a lot of blues playing. Since this lick is specifically for the A chord, you can use it only in the blues progression where the A chord is present. It won't fit over the IV and V chords.

FIGURE 14-2 uses double stops, meaning you play two notes at a time. This lick uses the A-minor pentatonic scale with added ninth and sixth. At the end, this lick uses another major third of C♯ to help round out the sound.

FIGURE 14-3 uses the A-Major triad (A, C♯, E) and slides from above and below certain pitches. Using just those three notes with embellishment can make a nice phrase.

FIGURE 14-1 A pentatonic with added major third

TRACK 56

FIGURE 14-2 A-pentatonic double stops

TRACK 57

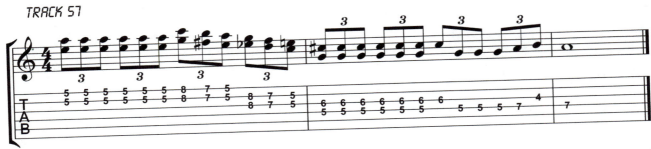

FIGURE 14-3 A arpeggio with slides

TRACK 58

FIGURE 14-4 A-Dorian blues riff

TRACK 59

FIGURE 14-5 A pentatonic with bend

TRACK 60

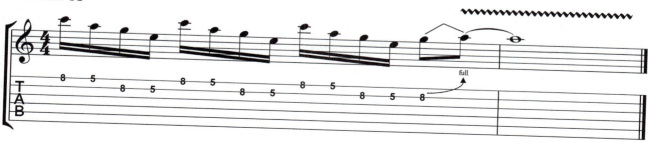

FIGURE 14-4 uses the A-Dorian scales as a replacement for the pentatonic scale. Notice the double stop and slide. Use the inflections often to spice up licks. Notice how the last note is an A, the strongest note in the key.

The last lick in the key of A is a simple repetitive lick using the top two strings of an A-minor pentatonic scale with a bend at the end—simple, but effective. See FIGURE 14-5.

Blues Solo Riffs in E

Using the E-minor pentatonic scale in the open or first position is a staple of great blues players including Stevie Ray Vaughan. FIGURE 14-6 is a simple but powerful lick in the open position using a chromatic passing tone for spice.

FIGURE 14-7 shows a pentatonic blues lick using bends and also utilizing a B-fifth passing tone taken from the blues scale.

You can apply arpeggios to the blues with great results. Since the blues is often based on dominant seventh chords, you can play dominant seventh arpeggios to match. The lick in FIGURE 14-8 simply ascends up an E-seventh arpeggio and descends with the Dorian scale.

Using chromatic notes to "fill in" the spaces between the pentatonic scales can yield some fresh sounds. FIGURE 14-9 shows an E pentatonic with chromatic tones to fill in the intervals.

 FIGURE 14-6   Open position, E pentatonic

TRACK 61

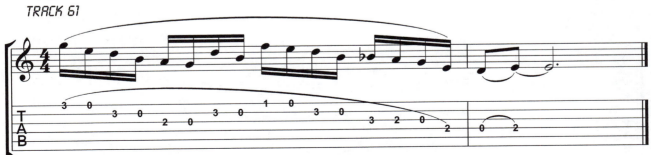

FIGURE 14-7   E pentatonic with bends

TRACK 62

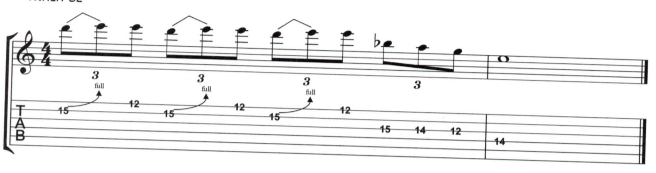

FIGURE 14-8   E-seventh riff ascending, E Dorian descending

TRACK 63

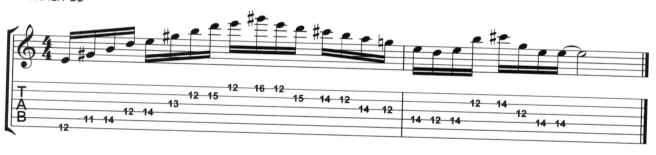

FIGURE 14-9   E-pentatonic scale with chromatic tones

TRACK 64

FIGURE 14-10   E-Mixolydian scale riff

TRACK 65

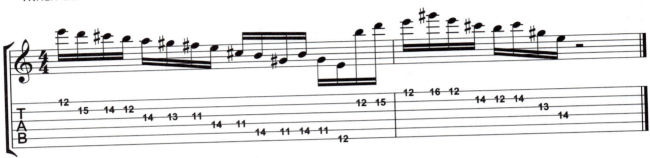

FIGURE 14-11   A blues with extended chords

TRACK 66

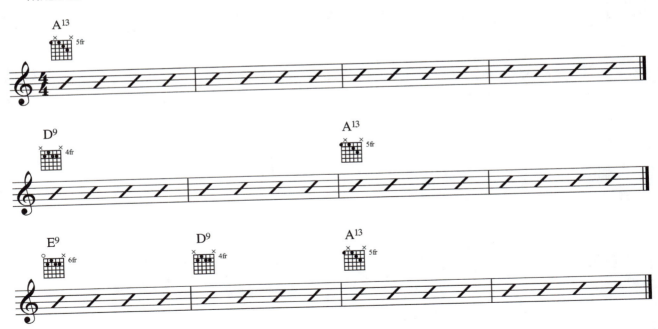

The last riff in E utilizes the Mixolydian mode in place of the pentatonic scale for E blues. (See **FIGURE 14-10**.) Since this scale matches up with the E-seventh chord found so often in the blues, you can use this to vary your sound. The lick is simply a rearrangement of the scale tones.

Blues Rhythm and Chord Sets

In addition to the shuffle pattern found in Chapter 2, there is a lot more you can do with the standard twelve-bar blues progression by adding other chords. In Chapter 8 you learned about extended chords that can be used in blues. The next four examples use different extended chords to add spice to your blues chordal playing.

The example in **FIGURE 14-11** uses simple extended chords through an A blues.

FIGURE 14-12   E blues with extended chords

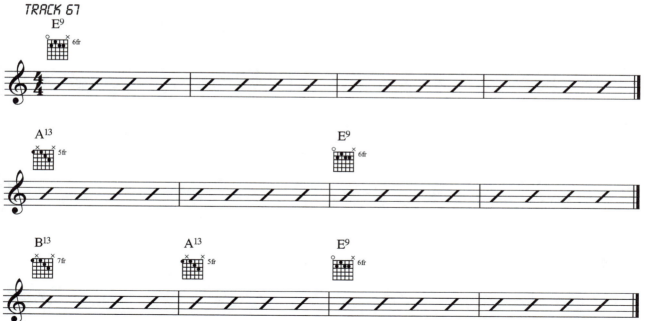

If you change keys to E, you see that the chord shapes stay the same, but they're used in a different context. A lot of this depends on where the root of the I chord is: with the key of E, it's easier to use a fifth string root. In the key of A, it is easier for a sixth string root. It all depends on what key you're in. See **FIGURE 14-12**.

When you're faced with E seventh, remember that any chord or chords from the family of dominant chords will do. In the case of E seventh, any of the dominant chords and extensions will work (E seventh, E ninth, E thirteenth, and so on).

Borrowing a tip from jazz, you can add a very dissonant chord right at the end of the fourth measure. While you're changing only one chord, that dissonance makes a big difference. The example in **FIGURE 14-13** is also in E.

The next chordal example (shown in **FIGURE 14-14**) is based on the minor blues form. This form isn't used as often as the standard twelve-bar

FIGURE 14-13   E blues with dissonant chord added

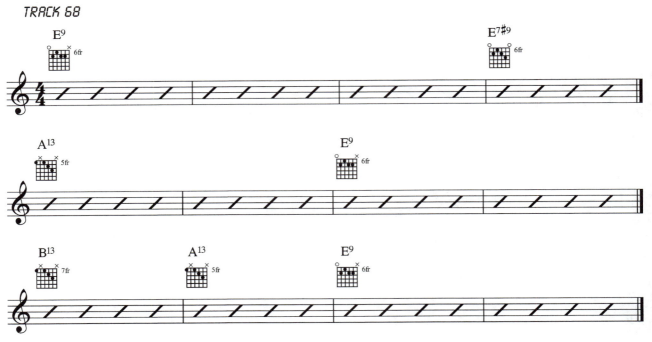

FIGURE 14-14   A-minor blues progression

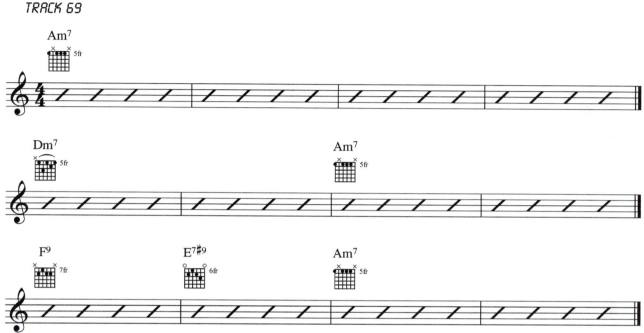

TRACK 69

blues, but B.B. King used it in "The Thrill Is Gone" with great success. Notice the nice extended chords that help round out the harmony.

Blues Turnarounds and Ending Lines

At the end of the blues progression on the twelfth bar there is what's known as a turnaround. Usually, it's an extra chord used to help the blues progression turn around and start again. At that point in the progression, many players play signature licks and lines to help the solo turn around as well. There are many of these licks, and they can be used during a solo or at the very end of the tune.

To start with, let's look at a blues progression with a turnaround chord so you can hear the sound of a turnaround. See **FIGURE 14-15**. The extra V chord helps the progression start over because of the pull it creates.

There are some very cliché lines that blues guitar players all know. When you solo, you should know them, too. **FIGURE 14-16** shows a lick for the last two bars of an A blues. This simple descending lick is based on the interval of a major sixth that falls chromatically down the fingerboard.

FIGURE 14-17 shows the same idea of falling intervals, this time based on a minor third, this time in E.

FIGURE 14-15   A blues with turnaround chord

TRACK 70

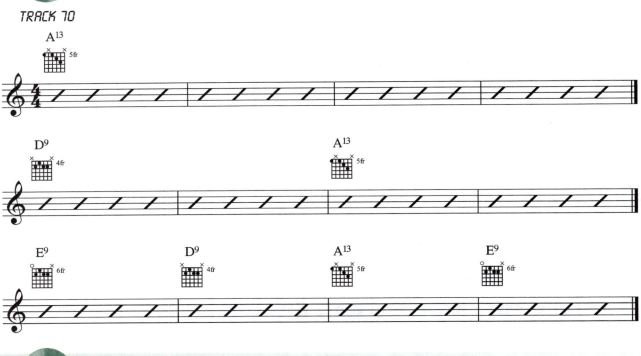

FIGURE 14-16   Falling sixths in A

TRACK 71

The next two examples (see **FIGURES 14-18** and **14-9**) will make the finger-style fans happy, because they show two ending lines that can be played finger style to end a blues lick. They are also based on the falling sixth interval but include a pedal tone, which is a note that is repeated through the figure. One is in A and one is in E.

FIGURE 14-17   Falling thirds in E

TRACK 72

FIGURE 14-18   Finger-style ending line in A

TRACK 73

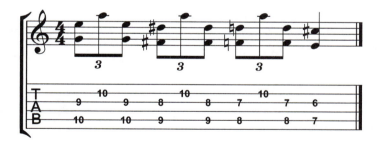

FIGURE 14-19   Finger-style ending line in E

TRACK 74

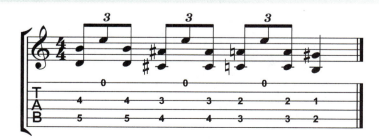

Conclusions

The lines and licks that appear in this chapter aren't the be-all, end-all of music. They serve as a basis from which you can learn the language of music. As you study your favorite players, learn the lines that you enjoy and integrate them into your playing. Above all else, try to create your own lines and phrases. Blues is music that can't easily be broken down into licks—although there are a few clichés that everyone knows. The emphasis is on improvisation and creation. Have fun. Ⓔ

Chapter 15

Putting It All Together: Rock and Beyond

The genre of rock music is hard to generalize, because the wealth of creativity and unique approaches that are a part of rock music make it a very broad topic indeed. Modern rock tends to be a mishmash of different styles and techniques. This chapter combines techniques, chords, scales, and other musical elements you learned in previous chapters to show you how to be creative with the basic elements of music.

Endless Options

Rock music isn't as clear-cut as the blues. The blues is based on repeating chords, so applying chords and solos to the blues is simple because of its repeating nature. Rock has no common traits—every artist and group does something a little different. While it's true that early rock stemmed from blues, and shares some common traits with that genre, the evolution of rock music has taken no specific direction. Almost anything goes. You can turn any of the chords and keys you learned in earlier chapters into riffs for songs and solo ideas. Rock music, especially modern rock music, manifests itself in many different keys. So, unlike the last chapter on blues, this chapter shows examples spread across a spectrum of keys.

Pentatonic Riffs and Solo Ideas

The pentatonic scale is a multipurpose scale, and it can be used effectively for creating riffs, or as a soloing tool. **FIGURE 15-1** shows a riff based completely on the A-minor pentatonic scale. Notice how only the bottom five notes are used—making for a catchy lick.

As a soloing tool, no scale has had more use than the minor pentatonic scale. **FIGURE 15-2** shows a typical looping lick used by many players. It includes a bend with some string skipping through an E-minor pentatonic scale.

A sequence refers to a pattern; or an order in which to play a scale.

FIGURE 15-1   A-minor pentatonic riff

TRACK 75

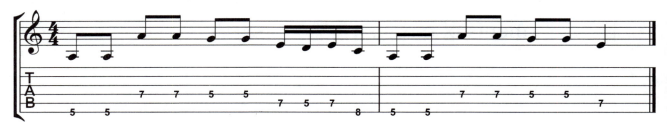

We can apply a sequence to a scale with some very cool results. Using a D-minor pentatonic scale based on a sequence, you can make a long sequential lick, as shown in **FIGURE 15-3**. Eric Johnson is famous for these kinds of lines.

FIGURE 15-2   E-minor pentatonic scale, looping with bend

TRACK 76

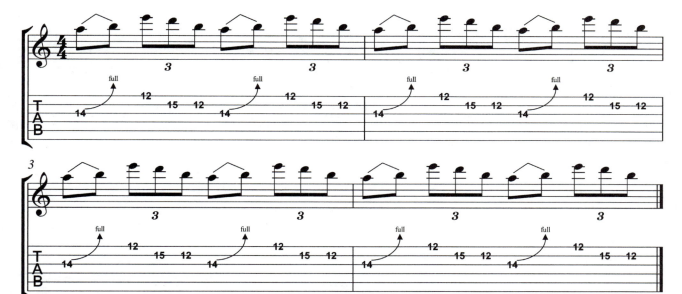

FIGURE 15-3   D-minor pentatonic scale sequence

TRACK 77

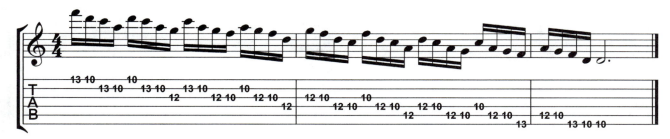

FIGURE 15-4 uses a G-minor pentatonic scale spanning the entire neck, played solely on the first two strings. This is also an effective way to take the scale out of its "box" and stretch it across the neck.

FIGURE 15-4   G-minor pentatonic scale on first two strings

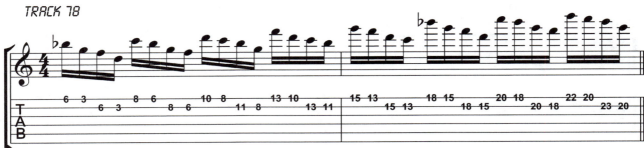

TRACK 78

FIGURE 15-5   G-Major scale sequence

TRACK 79

Major and Minor Scale Ideas

Sequences are a great way of elongating licks. Sequences can be any combination of notes that you like; you set the formula. You can apply a simple four-note pattern to a G-Major scale and play it all over the neck. **FIGURE 15-5** shows an effective and long scale run that holds together due to its regular pattern.

Scales can be broken up with large interval skips. **FIGURE 15-6** shows a sequence that utilizes perfect fourth interval skips.

For the minor scale, you can apply intervals using thirds throughout the scale. Using repetitive ideas like this can help the scale sound cohesive—and not like one long, boring scale. See **FIGURE 15-7**.

FIGURE 15-6 A-Major scale with interval skips

TRACK 80

FIGURE 15-7 D-minor scale in thirds

TRACK 81

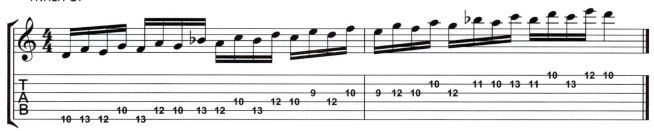

FIGURE 15-8 shows an unusual example of an E-minor scale played completely on the first string. By using every other note as an open string, you can create what classical musicians refer to as a "pedal point," which is a repeating note you keep coming back to. Angus Young from AC/DC used this technique on the song "Thunderstruck."

The Modes

Dorian, Mixolydian, Lydian, and Phrygian are the most common modes, so these are the ones shown in the examples that follow. The hardest part is accentuating the individual flavor of each mode. Remember, each

FIGURE 15-8   E-minor pedal-point scale

TRACK 82

FIGURE 15-9   C-Dorian example

TRACK 83

one of these modes differs from traditional major and minor scales by only one note, and that note needs to be emphasized.

FIGURE 15-9 uses the Dorian scale in C. Notice how the note A (the sharp sixth) is emphasized in this lick.

The Mixolydian and its characteristic ♭ seventh can be a difficult scale to play. Try the example in **FIGURE 15-10** with string skipping through a G-Mixolydian mode to get your wheels turning.

You can take the idea of a pedal point and apply it to an E-Lydian mode. This time the pedal point is the highest note of the scale and the lick descends. See **FIGURE 15-11**.

FIGURE 15-10   G-Mixolydian example with string skipping

TRACK 84

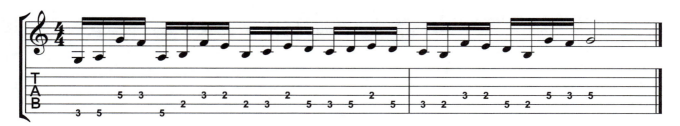

FIGURE 15-11   E Lydian, pedal point descending

TRACK 85

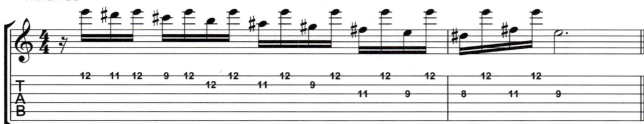

FIGURE 15-12 A Phrygian in octaves

TRACK 86

FIGURE 15-13 C-Major diatonic arpeggios

TRACK 87

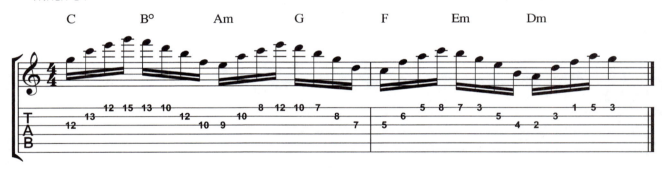

FIGURE 15-14 E-minor arpeggio across neck

TRACK 88

For the Phrygian mode, the focus in **FIGURE 15-12** is on the B second interval found in this scale. The entire lick is played in octaves as a double-note run. Many players use octaves to strengthen their single note playing.

Arpeggios

Besides playing individual arpeggios just over chords, you can stretch them out to scales. By playing all of the arpeggios found in a key you can play simple scales in extraordinary ways. Here is a C-Major scale played in arpeggios. Note in **FIGURE 15-13** what chords are utilized.

You can also stretch one arpeggio all over the neck by repeating the notes on every string. Try to repeat an E-minor triad (E, G, B) as many times as possible on the neck. Try the example in **FIGURE 15-14** to get you started.

Tapping

Now you get to have fun with tapping. Let's apply it to a pentatonic scale extending the scale from two notes on every string to three notes per string. The taps are used for the third note on each string. Try **FIGURE 15-15** the next time you play a D-minor pentatonic scale.

FIGURE 15-15   D-minor pentatonic with taps

TRACK 89

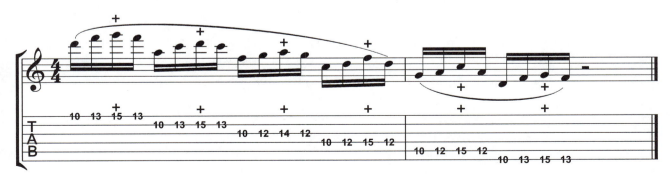

FIGURE 15-16 D-minor pentatonic with large interval tap

TRACK 90

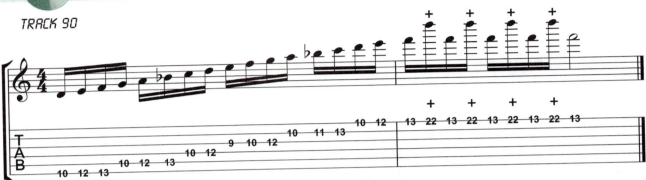

Tapping is also great for flashy licks. Try the next example of a D-minor scale that ascends and then taps at the top. The catch is, the tap is the highest note of most guitars (the twenty-second fret D). The large interval sounds unexpected and also makes the lick unplayable any other way. See **FIGURE 15-16**.

Combinations Licks

You can combine some of the single elements, such as chords, techniques, and other musical elements, to make useful runs. To start, you can easily combine scales and arpeggios as shown in the next example, which ascends through a major scale and descends with an arpeggio. If you like to sweep, you can sweep the descending arpeggios—be creative! See **FIGURE 15-17**.

Here is another scale/arpeggio combination. This time you can intersperse the scale and arpeggio more freely throughout the example. Notice that you have to play only a few notes of a scale and a few notes of an arpeggio before moving on to the next one. See **FIGURE 15-18**.

You can also combine techniques, such as tapping and bending, for unusual effects. The example in **FIGURE 15-19** of a lick in A minor taps a note and then bends the string with the left hand causing the pitch of the tapped note to rise. It's a very cool effect!

FIGURE 15-17 C-Major scale ascending, C-Major arpeggio descending

TRACK 91

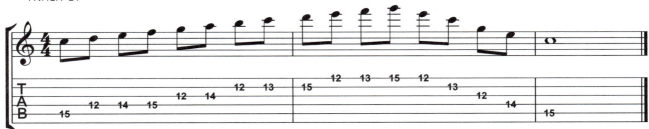

FIGURE 15-18 G-Major scale/arpeggio combination

TRACK 92

FIGURE 15-19 A-minor bend/tap

TRACK 93

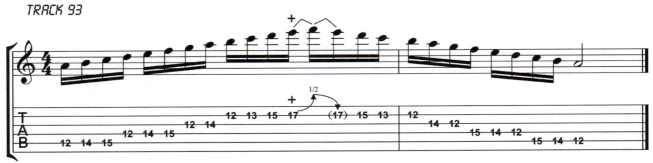

FIGURE 15-20 B-Major-seventh arpeggio with tap slide

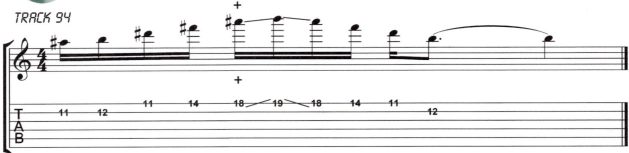

FIGURE 15-21 E-minor mega example

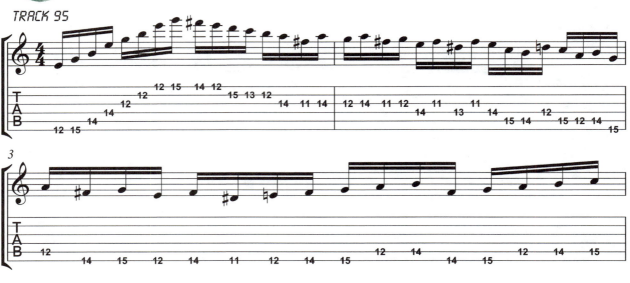

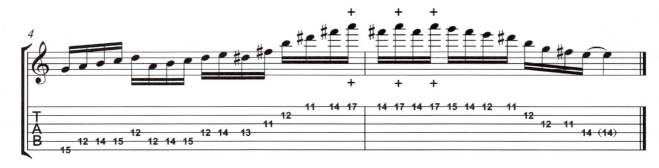

Here's a fun way to tap, called a tap slide. Instead of just tapping one note, you can slide the tap finger up or down a fret. In **FIGURE 15-20** the tap slide is applied to a B-Major-seventh arpeggio using the tap for the notes A♯ and B of the arpeggio.

Conclusions

When studying this chapter, learn the elements of each lick and try to apply them elsewhere. Elements like sequence, pedal points, and intervals can be applied to any musical situation. Try to use the examples in this chapter as a launching pad for your own imagination. To finish, let's do a monster lick in E minor. See **FIGURE 15-21**. This lick includes sequence, arpeggios, intervals, and tapping in one mega example.

As you study great guitar solos you'll notice that the players use the techniques and other musical elements that you've learned, and combine them freely to make lines. Don't be a passive listener. When you hear something you like, go back and study it to find out what makes it work. Then you'll be able to understand it and use it in your own way, without copying it exactly. As you can see from this chapter, there's no end to the combinations you can make from elements like scales and arpeggios and chords, and turn into great music.

Chapter 16

Playing by Ear

Since music is an art of sound, being able to hear and use your ears effectively is very important. Ear training involves the subtle art of hearing, and by strengthening your ears you become a more acute listener, which will help you in all aspects of playing the guitar. There's no right or exact way to hear, and you have to make judgments for yourself. When it comes down to it, ear training is an amazing art.

Perfect Pitch vs. Relative Pitch

Guitar is an instrument that rewards those who can listen well. How do we start to improve our ears? How can you practice this aspect that some seem to have and some don't? First, I'll discuss the differences between perfect pitch and relative pitch.

Perfect pitch is the ability to hear a note and name it by pitch. It's something you're born with or you acquire at a very early age, most often before the age of five or six. Perfect pitch is very rare and if you weren't born with it, you'll never have true perfect pitch. Someone with perfect pitch can name even the pitch of cars going by, airplanes flying above, and heel clicks down below!

Perfect pitch is not always a blessing. To some, it can be a nightmare that hurts their ability to simply listen to music without analyzing.

You don't have to have perfect pitch to be a great listener or to play by ear. The rest of us use relative pitch, which entails being able to hear the relationships between notes. It's the ability to recognize something you hear as simply a major scale or a major chord, instead of specifically a C-Major scale (as someone with perfect pitch can do). Relative pitch can be sharpened to an exacting detail, and players with heightened senses of relative pitch can rival those with perfect pitch.

Beginning Your Ear Training

Every guitar player has some experience with playing by ear. Whether you tried to match the sound of a song, or you were able to correct a mistake in an online tab because it didn't sound correct, you were using your ears acutely for both. To start training your ear, listen to the broad categories of music theory—the roots of chords, types of scales, and types of chords.

The first thing to do is try to match a single note. It would really help if you could get a guitar-playing friend to help you with this, and then you could quiz each other. If you don't have a friend who plays guitar, don't worry. Almost anyone can muster up enough ability to play one note on the guitar—even someone who doesn't play. You could also ask your teacher to help you with this exercise.

To start with, have someone play a note on a certain string and tell you what string it's played on. (This isn't a guessing game—you won't be able to tell one note name from another unless you have perfect pitch, but you can tell how far apart the notes are.) When you start, see if you can tell if you are too high or too low. You're not going to know exactly how far away, but if you can narrow the direction you have to move, you're starting to hear more acutely.

Be patient and try to get as close as you can to the note. Your first few attempts may not yield much success, but like anything else you've studied, you need to practice to get good at it. Keep trying different notes and different strings. Some students hear better in certain ranges of the guitar, and that is normal.

As you keep doing these exercises, listen for the important factors of how high or low you are and how far you should move back. If you can get it down to two or three tries, you're doing very well.

ALERT!

Don't make the mistake of believing you have to start at the beginning of a song. You should start wherever you're comfortable starting. Start where you can succeed! Ear training is a slow process and can be quite frustrating. Just remember that being able to learn a new song is akin to learning how to play fast and clean—neither one happens without practice. Try to practice ear training each day when you play.

Hearing Power Chords

To take this exercise to the next step, ask your friend to play a power chord with a root on either the sixth or fifth string. Do the same procedure that you did for the single notes, but this time use power chords instead of single notes. Listen to how high or low you are and where you think you should move. As you get better at this, ask your friend to play a few chords at a time. As you get used to hearing it this way, you'll develop a memory for what you hear.

If you're succeeding at this exercise, especially with multiple chords, move on to real songs. Start cracking away at the songs you've always wanted to learn but can't find in tabs anywhere. Some players find that they can learn only small parts of songs at first, and this is normal. At the beginning stages, you'll be able to accomplish only a little bit each day. In a short time, you will get the song in full.

Hearing Major and Minor Chords

Your first step when listening to major and minor chords is to identify which chord you are hearing. Major chords sound happy and minor chords sound sad. This may sound childish but it works—try it and you will see. Once you know what kind of chord (also called "quality" of chord) you have (major or minor), see if you can hear the root. Let's use D minor for an example. Once you figure out the quality of the chord (minor) you can use your guitar to find out which note is the root D. Ear training involves the subtle art of hearing. There is no right or exact way to hear and you have to make judgments for yourself. When it comes down to it, ear training is an amazing art.

Longer Melodies

The next step is to play back longer melodies of three or more notes. As you progress, you'll be able to judge how far away the next note is. Try upping the ante every day and increasing the number of notes you play back. Try picking out simple melodies like "Happy Birthday" and "Silent Night," or other familiar songs. Everything is game and everything is good! The more time you spend doing this the better!

Recognizing Scales

Being able to recognize the sound of a scale can help you figure out melodies. If you can tell that the melody is a major scale, this greatly narrows the note choices because you use the fingerings of scales you already know. Classical music is a great place to start because many times the title of the piece will give you the key and scale. It's common to see a title like "Opus 1 in A minor."

Listening to music in a scale that's already identified for you will help you to identify the sound of each scale. Major and minor scales, like their chordal counterparts, sound unique and are hard to mistake for one another. To train your ear, you can ask almost any musician to play you a scale. Just about every player who has studied another instrument will know both major and minor scales and will be able to play them for you.

FACT

When learning solos, especially rock and blues solos, you need to know what key you're in. As long as you can figure out what key the solo is in, you can place the appropriate scale in either major or minor. For example, if you know that the solo is in A, but you're unsure whether to use major or minor pentatonic, try to play an A-Major and an A-minor chord to tell for sure. Ninety percent of the rock solos that use pentatonic use the minor pentatonic scale.

Advanced Ear Training

Advanced ear training is the goal of any musician. Being able to hear the broad categories of theory, like what scale you are in, is fine. However, fine-tuning your ability to hear intervals will help you figure out melodies and solos with greater ease.

Intervals were covered at great length in Chapters 7, 8, 9, and 10, but we spoke about them as they related to scales. Now we can go back and relate intervals to guitar fingerings and, most important, to sounds. The first step is interval identification, which entails being able to hear the distance between two notes and then relating the distance to a fingering on guitar. Melodies are nothing more than long strings of intervals, and if you can hear the intervals, you'll be able to play what you hear with greater accuracy and ease.

Interval I.D.

Here's a trick for training yourself to hear and identify intervals. Select an interval in a familiar song and find out it's name; then listen for that same interval in other songs. When you hear it again, you'll already know what that interval is called. For example, the first two notes of "Here Comes the Bride" are a perfect fourth. When you hear that interval in other songs, you'll know you're hearing a perfect fourth. By using little tricks like this, you can learn to hear and label what you hear. In time, you won't need other songs to compare to—you will be able to just hear the intervals as they are.

For simplicity's sake, the examples that follow use C as the root for the intervals, and a few common fingerings. These do not represent all of the possible choices, but your knowledge of the fingerboard and the chord charts presented throughout this book will help you if you wish to look at the total picture.

Minor and Major Seconds

Minor seconds are the distance of one fret on the guitar. While you can play them across two strings, it is more common to play them on the same string since you are playing just two frets next to each other. Minor-second intervals are easy to hear because they're the smallest interval in Western music. A popular song based on the minor second interval is the theme from *Jaws*. **FIGURE 16-1** shows several minor seconds played across the guitar. Listen for the big fish!

FIGURE 16-1   Minor seconds

Major seconds are the distance of two frets on the guitar. Commonly you play these on any one single string, but you can play them across two strings. The song associated with this interval is the first interval of "Happy Birthday." **FIGURE 16-2** shows major seconds played across the guitar on both single strings and across two strings.

Minor thirds are the distance of three frets. The popular songs to help you are the first notes of "O Canada" and "Greensleeves." If these songs

FIGURE 16-2 Major seconds

FIGURE 16-3 Minor thirds

FIGURE 16-4 Major thirds

aren't familiar to you, then work on learning the sound of the interval from repetition. **FIGURE 16-3** shows an example with fingering.

Major thirds are the distance of four frets, and are commonly played across two strings; playing major thirds on a single string can be a real stretch. The song to help you is the beginning of "When the Saints Go Marching In." **FIGURE 16-4** shows an example with fingering.

Fourths and Fifths

Perfect fourths are the distance of five frets, and you rarely see them played across one string (that's a real reach). Perfect fourths are very easy to recognize because the songs based on them are so well-known. Perfect fourths start the song "Here Comes the Bride" and "Amazing Grace." **FIGURE 16-5** is an example with fingering.

Diminished fifths, also called tri-tones, are very distinct intervals.

FIGURE 16-5 Perfect fourths

FIGURE 16-6 Tri-tones

They can be tricky to hear at first, but once you get the hang of them they're hard to miss. "Maria" from *West Side Story* is based on the tri-tone, as well as *The Simpsons* theme. **FIGURE 16-6** is an example with fingerings.

The perfect fifth is another strong and easy interval to recognize. You've probably played it quite often because it's the basis of your power chords. "Twinkle, Twinkle, Little Star" is based on the perfect fifth. See **FIGURE 16-7**.

Sixths, Sevenths, and Octaves

The minor sixth is one of the most difficult intervals to recognize because there are so few songs based on it. There's no common or familiar song that everyone will know for this interval; you'll just have to listen to the interval itself to hear it. See **FIGURE 16-8**.

The major sixth is based on the first two notes of the NBC theme song, and an old folk tune "My Bonnie." See **FIGURE 16-9**.

FIGURE 16-7 Perfect fifths

FIGURE 16-8 Minor sixths

FIGURE 16-9 Major sixths

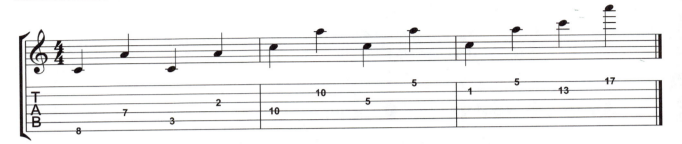

FIGURE 16-10 Minor sevenths

The minor seventh can be found in the theme song from *Star Trek: The Next Generation* and "A Place for Us" from *West Side Story*. See **FIGURE 16-10**.

The major seventh is very easy to hear because it sounds so dissonant—it's hard to miss. It's found in the "Theme from *Superman*," but you'll probably be able to identify this interval easily in any song. See **FIGURE 16-11**.

The last interval is the octave. It's used in "Somewhere Over the Rainbow." See **FIGURE 16-12**.

Being able to identify intervals will do wonders for your playing. We all find ourselves in situations where we have to play new music and sometimes this happens on the gig. If you're not a great sight-reader, you can compensate by having a great ear and being able to play exactly what you hear.

FIGURE 16-11 Major sevenths

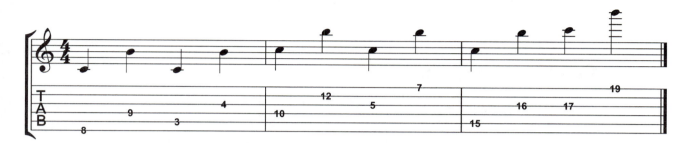

FIGURE 16-12 Octaves

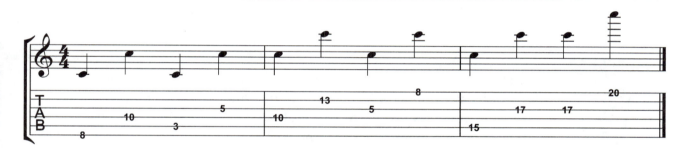

Transcribing

Transcribing is the art of writing down musical information for the sake of study. As you know, learning solos, licks, and lines from your favorite players is some of the most valuable practice time that you can spend. There's a difference between playing someone's solo and learning from it. Learning to transcribe by ear also helps you to learn the solo. It's not necessary to learn it all note for note at the correct speed. It's fine to learn a few licks and write them down for future study. Either way you do it, you should write it down on tablature or music paper so you can study it.

If you're really interested in learning about music, you should check out how other instruments play and phrase. In the case of blues, there are many piano and saxophone players to check out—harmonica players, too.

Other instruments won't fit into the box patterns as guitars do, but learning their licks will help you break out of the box. You'll often find that learning from other instruments can really turn your playing toward a new path.

Computer Help

The computer can be a powerful ally, especially when it comes to ear training. There are many wonderful computer programs that can drill you on all aspects of ear training. Some of the most popular programs are Ear Master, Practica Musica, and KAB. These pieces of software are set up to test your ability to recognize scales, chords, chord progressions, intervals, and much more. While none of them are tailored specifically to guitar, that doesn't matter because music is music, and ear training is the same for all instruments.

Sometimes just jamming away with your favorite records can be a great help. Not only will you have a great and steady accompaniment, you'll also be more aware of what keys the songs are played in, and what scales you can solo in.

The computer can also be a great deal of help when it comes to transcribing music by ear. There are programs with the ability to play a CD at a slower speed without changing the pitch. Popular programs are CD SlowDowner, Transkriber, and CD Looper. Older generations who wanted to slow music down had to drop the speed on their record players by one half, but the pitch also dropped one octave. These amazing programs also allow you to loop small sections over and over again to help you narrow down hard parts that need repeating.

Ear training is something that you must study every day. You must make it a lifelong goal. Start now and learn to develop your most important tool as a musician—your ears. All you need to unlock the secrets of your favorite players is good listening. Ⓔ

Chapter 17

How to Practice

For many, "practicing" may sound like a chore. But when you find an instrument that you enjoy playing, your yearning to improve will inspire your desire to practice. It's time to show you how to make the most of your time and practice like a pro. Common mistakes and pitfalls can be avoided and you can get to where you want!

The Meaning of "Practice"

Practice is defined as doing or performing something repeatedly in order to acquire or polish a skill. This is the simplest way to look at practicing, yet many students lump everything they do on the guitar into practicing. Just playing your guitar isn't practicing; it's more akin to reinforcing old habits. Many students believe that they practice a lot and are very efficient, when in reality they end up spinning their wheels more than they are actually learning.

The truth is that practicing—true practicing—is very hard work and shouldn't last for long periods of time. When you hear of friends gloating about their eight-hour marathon practice sessions, you have every right to be suspicious. Most guitar players don't really understand what practice really involves, and most seem to equate time spent playing the guitar with practice time. Practicing involves working on one thing at a time— one specific weakness—and working on it until you get it right. True practicing is focused, organized work, and it shouldn't be measured in hours or minutes. The amount of time spent cannot quantify your improvement.

Get Organized

Time management is the most crucial aspect to improving. It doesn't matter how much time you have every day; what matters is how you spend that time. Ten minutes of focused daily practice beats four hours of marathon practice once a week. So, first things first, you need to develop a schedule.

If you tend to make up for lost time with long sessions, you need to rethink your approach. You can compare practicing to training for the Olympics. You wouldn't expect an Olympic athlete to train only one day a week, would you? Playing every day, even for only a few minutes, is more beneficial in the long run than inconsistent long practice.

Routine is the key. You want guitar practice to be part of your daily routine, just like brushing your teeth. It's part of your daily routine, and you get used to doing it. Even though it's a bad idea to quantify practice in minutes, a good one-hour slot is a nice place to start. What are you going to practice for one hour? The answer is, many small things, because you need to keep your practice sessions interesting and lively to help break up the monotony.

Know Thyself

Part of this game is understanding what to practice. Some of us are lucky enough to see our weaknesses, but others have no idea where to start. Here are the categories that everyone should practice on a regular basis, along with some of the possibilities for practice in each category:

- *Scales*—including major, minor, modes, and pentatonic
- *Arpeggios*—either learning fingerings or applying them to musical situations
- *Technique*—practicing *anything* is a technique exercise
- Chords—learning a new voicing, working on progressions, or songwriting
- *Ear training*—including interval identification and chord identification
- *Musicianship*—including sight-reading, fingerboard knowledge, and anything else you can think of!

FACT

John Petrucci of Dream Theater is one of the most disciplined guitar players around. His approach to practicing is very logical and organized. He uses a filing cabinet filled with folders for various musical subjects, with musical examples to practice for each. When it comes time to do a practice session, he just selects music from each folder and works on those for that session. Doing the same will ensure you get a well-rounded education.

The Basics

For technical work use a metronome. The importance of a metronome can't be stressed enough—it's the most valuable tool you have. Not only will it allow you to gradually increase the difficulty of your practice routines, it will also help you play in time better. Any musician will tell you that being able to keep great time, not rushing or dragging, is one of the most important traits you can have.

You also should find a quiet and comfortable space to practice. Turn your phone off; log off your online service. Try to get a solid hour with no distractions. Sit in a comfortable chair. Make a nice space for yourself. You should be comfortable there—mood lighting helps too.

No matter what you practice, you need to start slowly and work up the speed. Trying to play too fast just reinforces mistakes. If you have a difficult passage, slow it down and figure out what parts give you problems. Once you identify the trouble sections, work on those separately. It's quite normal for musicians to work on small chunks of music and later work on the whole piece. If you have a trouble spot, drill it until you get it right.

And finally, keep a logbook or a practice journal, and keep track of what you did and how long you did it.

Practicing Scales

If there's anything that scares students, it's scale practice. By now, you understand the importance of what scales can do for your playing. Maybe you've read through the shapes and thought they sounded pretty cool. So how do you practice scales? First of all, don't worry about technique or playing fast, because your only goal here is to learn the shapes and how to use them, nothing else. Scales can be broken down into four subcategories: major, minor, major pentatonic, and minor pentatonic.

Here's where the fun comes in. Get five bowls from your kitchen and a package of index cards. Start with a stack of twelve index cards, and write a note name on each card. Since there are twelve chromatic notes in music, you'll have a card for each note. Put that stack into one of the bowls; these cards will provide the root of the scale you will practice. Next, make up cards for the fingerings of the minor and major scales— one set of six cards for the major scale; one set of six cards for the minor scale (six fingerings for each from Chapter 6). Place one set in each of two bowls. Then, make up cards with the shapes for the pentatonic scales—one set of five cards for the major pentatonic, and one set of five for the minor pentatonic (five shapes for both from Chapter 5). Place one set in each of the two remaining bowls. When you go to practice scales, pick one card from the bowl that contains the twelve notes. This will tell you what key to play the scales in. Then pick one other card from any of the four remaining bowls. You may end up playing the E♭ Major scale on the fifth string one day, or the G♯ minor pentatonic scale, form II shape, the next day.

This is just one way to approach practicing scales, but the nice part is the built-in variety. If you really want to learn certain scales first, go ahead and start on those first. Try to internalize the scales by playing them up and down, backwards and forwards. Use your imagination to come up with different ways to play them. You may come up with a great riff from this! Or, to spice things up you can just pick a card from the bowl of note names and practice every scale from that root. For example, if you pull out the root D, try playing every D scale you can think of—major, minor, pentatonic major, and pentatonic minor.

The maximum time you should spend practicing scales is about one hour. One hour is a long time to really work on something. The minimum is twenty minutes.

What you're trying to learn here is not only how to play the shapes, but also how to place the shapes into different keys. Don't worry about licks and riffs; once you know the shapes like the back of your hand, you'll be in a much better position to make up riffs and licks of your own.

Practicing Arpeggios

You can use the same index card technique for practicing arpeggios. You can reuse the bowl with the roots, but start a new pile of cards for all the different arpeggio patterns you learned in this book. If you've learned other arpeggios from other sources, add them to the pot, too. Since the arpeggios are linked to chords, it's a good idea to practice them through some standard progressions. And yes, you can make cards for progressions, too. Use the twelve-bar blues and the I-vi-IV-V progressions, and if you have chord progressions from your songs, go ahead and use them, too. Mix it up and select different things every day. Practicing this way will keep your brain constantly challenged; plus, this is one of the best ways to learn the fingerboard because you're constantly moving shapes around.

Practicing Modes

There are seven modes and seven days in a week—do one a day, and mix up the roots. If you're already practicing major and minor scales you can cut out two modes, because the Ionian mode is another name for the major scale, and Aeolian mode is another name for the minor. You practice modes for the same reason you practice any other scale—if you don't have the shapes down cold you'll have a difficult time using them effectively. Once the shapes are internalized you can start using them. Practicing scales doesn't have to be boring; try spending some time just playing modes over tunes.

Refer to Chapter 10 for sample tunes that contain modal progressions. You can disguise practicing for soloing by practicing it over a recording! As long as you use the song to explore the different fingerings that are possible, there is absolutely nothing wrong with this. You will be getting a chance to play with great players. The drummer will take the place of the metronome, so you can work on your timing, too. Many players practice their scales this way.

Practicing Technique

The techniques for posture and playing correctly are covered in Chapter 11. You should be comfortable with these aspects of technique first, and then move on to extended techniques covered in Chapter 12. Too many players tend to place too much importance on playing fast without realizing that the way to play faster is to develop good technique first. Having good technique allows you to play anything, and that's why you should develop it.

Picking-Hand Problems

The picking hand has three challenges that come up time and time again. People tend to have a hard time learning string-skipping, string-crossing, and upstroking. No matter what you try to play, whether it's a scale or an arpeggio, gaining mastery of these elements will serve you well; the following exercises should help you to do just that.

String-skipping refers to playing notes on nonadjacent strings. Because your pick has to make large jumps, it can be hard to control. **FIGURE 17-1** shows a simple string-skipping exercise using an open-position E-Major chord.

FIGURE 17-1   String-skipping exercise

String-crossing involves changing strings when you alternate-pick. If your last pick was a down pick, then when you cross strings, your next pick will have to be an upstroke. Try the example in **FIGURE 17-2** to see what it feels like.

Because your pick has to travel quite a distance to the other side of the string for the upstroke, this is typically a hard movement and can really hang you up on fast alternate-picked scales. **FIGURE 17-3** is a great example to work on. Watch the picking carefully!

The only reason that most players find upstrokes difficult is because upstrokes aren't used a lot. Most rhythm playing is done with down strokes, and most licks and examples in this book start with down strokes, too. So, if you were to make a mistake in alternate-picking, it would probably be to play two down strokes in a row. To correct yourself, you can try two things. First, try to start licks with upstrokes

FIGURE 17-2   String-crossing exercise

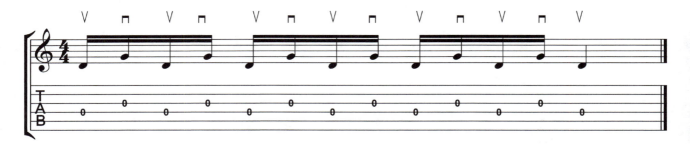

FIGURE 17-3   String-crossing exercise

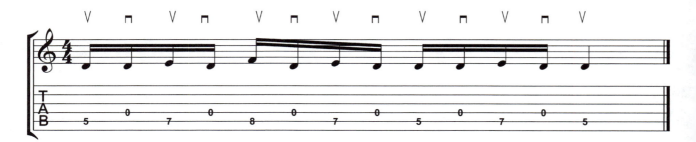

and continue to alternate-pick from there. You can also try to play with just upstrokes for just a few minutes, although it's very fatiguing, so don't overdo it. After doing a minute or so on this, go back to alternate-picking to see how much more comfortable you are now.

The Fretting Hand

If you play slowly and synchronize both hands, the fretting hand gets to come along for the ride. If you're playing clean scales and everything sounds good, then don't worry. But for a lot of players, getting their fingers to work independently is the hardest thing. **FIGURE 17-4** is a drill to kick those fingers into shape. Watch the fingerings—they are vital to success.

With the exception of your fingers, which might need help with an independence exercise, your fret hand should naturally strengthen from practicing scales and arpeggios. If you believe that your hands have a problem in a certain area, the best way to attack that problem is to slow the problem down and keep working through it till you conquer it.

FIGURE 17-4 Finger independence exercise

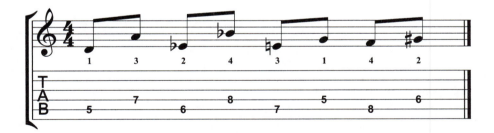

Practicing Chords

Chordal practice is a little hard to pin down; many players learn a lot just by playing their favorite songs. If you're interested in expanding your chord knowledge, you can try one of those huge chord books with 17.2 billion chords in them, and try to learn a new chord each week.

A more realistic goal is to figure out more voicings of the chords you already know, and work on those.

You can use the fingerboard charts to plot out the notes and try new chords, or you can randomly put your hands on the guitar and try to name the chord. If you're a beginner having trouble switching chords, slow down the motion and switch the chords twenty times in a row without mistake. If you can do any task twenty times in a row without mistake, you can say that you know it. There are always lots of things to study with chords, so don't think that after you know all the chords in this book you're done. We've only scratched the surface of chords. Chords and harmony on the guitar is a lifelong study. Appendix A lists resources for some great chord books.

Sight-reading is one area of musicianship that many guitar players overlook. There's an old joke that goes like this: "How do you get guitar players to stop playing? Put sheet music in front of them." While it *is* possible to learn guitar just by listening and memorizing, learning to read music will open up many new doors of opportunity to you.

Chapter 18

Sound and Gear

The world of guitar is filled with toys. Open up any guitar magazine and you're hit with page after page of advertisements for new pedals, guitars, strings, and anything else you can think of. The world of guitar equipment isn't that confusing after all, and with a little knowledge, you can become a budding gearhead and informed user/buyer.

Electric Guitars

Contrary to popular belief, there are only two types of electric guitars on the market—Fender style and the Gibson style; everything else is an adaptation of those two. While there are many other manufacturers to choose from, the seeds planted by these two companies in the 1950s have provided the basic model of what a guitar should be.

Fender Style

In early 1954, Leo Fender released the Fender Stratocaster and started a revolution. While this wasn't the first electric guitar ever produced, it was revolutionary in its mass-market appeal and classic styling, and has undergone little change since. The Strat consists of a wooden body, with a separate neck that is attached to the body by four long bolts. This style of construction is called "bolt-on" neck construction, and this innovation allowed Fender to reduce the prices of its guitars for the mass market. The bolt-on neck is still used today and is a staple of the Fender style. The Strat is designed with three single-coil pickups, a five-way pickup switch, tremolo system, volume knob, and two tone knobs for its electronics system. Its body design is contoured to fit your body and includes cutaways for both hands to play comfortably. Fender now produces various Strat models, but the standard Stratocaster remains virtually unchanged. Countless manufacturers have replicated this design.

FACT

Famous Stratocaster players include Jimi Hendrix, Stevie Ray Vaughan, Eric Clapton, Jeff Beck, Ritchie Blackmore, David Gilmour, and Yngwie Malmsteen.

Gibson Style

The Gibson Les Paul, launched in 1952 and designed by guitar legend Les Paul, is the other dominant style in electric guitars. The design of the Les Paul is radically different from the Fender design. Even though the Strat made its first appearance in 1954, Fender was producing other electric guitars before then, and their designs influenced Les Paul's design.

The Les Paul is designed with a set neck that is glued in, which is one of the reasons the Les Paul has a different sound—the set neck helps the guitar sustain longer than the bolt-on Fender counterpart. The body style is also different from the Strat. Instead of having a solid flat top like the Strat, the Les Paul has a double-arch top comprised of two pieces of wood glued together. Unlike the Strat, the Les Paul includes only one cutaway for the fretting hand; and the electronics are very different—it contains only two pickups, and a three-way pickup switch. Each pickup has its own separate tone and volume knobs. The placement of the pickup switch is moved up toward the player's body. Because of their heavier construction and arch top, Les Pauls are considerably heavier than Stratocasters.

FACT

Some important Les Paul players are: Les Paul, Jimmy Page, Eric Clapton, Ace Frehley, Joe Walsh, and Joe Perry.

To Hum or Not to Hum

In the early days of pickup design, all guitars used single-coil pickups. These pickups had only one problem, they buzzed when amplified. The buzz came from the AC current, which alternates sixty times a second. The sensitive wires in the pickups heard this noise and reproduced it as slight buzz, or hum, when amplified. If you own a Strat and think your guitar is busted, think again; all single-coil pickups do this. In 1959, Seth Lover, an engineer at Gibson, set out on a battle to stop pickups from humming. Gibson figured out that if you place two single coils right next to each other and wire them together, they cancel out the hum. These pickups were named "humbuckers" because they stopped the hum. While this was a great triumph for guitar engineering, one thing changed as a result of these new pickups: the sound. The double pickups were louder and sounded different than the Strat's pickups. In 1959, Les Paul models included humbucking pickups as a standard item.

The Sound

In the 1950s, the Strat and the Les Paul sounded somewhat different from each other due to their different construction and wood types. With the introduction of the humbucking pickup in 1959, the difference between the two guitars became dramatic. The single-coil pickups found on Fender guitars, while they did exhibit an annoying buzz, had a clean glassy sound that was favored by many players. The Les Paul, with its humbuckers, had a richer and darker sound compared to the light twang of a Strat.

It became almost impossible to make the Strat sound like a Les Paul and vice versa. Certain styles of music started to rely on these sounds—the Fender found its way into country and rhythm and blues music, while the Les Paul was at home in jazz and rock music.

Super Guitars

Throughout the 1960s and 1970s, other guitar companies flooded the market with copies of the early Fender- and Gibson-style guitars. Even though Fender and Gibson started to vary their own lines, alternative Fender- and Gibson-style instruments started to hit the market. In the early 1980s, the guitar market saw the first "super guitars," instruments that borrowed style and components from the Strat guitars; they were "hot-rodded" with lighter bodies, and built with different electronic control options and body styles. The most notable "Super Strat" companies are Ibanez and Jackson.

If you're trying to emulate the sound of your favorite player, check into what type of guitar he or she uses, and get a guitar in the same family. It's hard to get a Stevie Ray Vaughan sound out of a Les Paul, because Vaughan's sound is defined by the sound of a Strat.

Both Fender and Gibson changed the guitar market. From these companies came such innovations as bolt-on necks, sharper, more contoured bodies, single coil pickups, humbucking pickups, and tremolos with locking systems to help keep the guitars in tune (an ailment that plagued Fender owners). Les Paul owners also found options in the super guitar market, most notably those made by guitar designer Paul Reed Smith (PRS), who took the basic theme of the Les Paul and sought to improve upon its design. PRS made lighter bodies (a typical Les Paul is around nine pounds) with double cutaways for more comfort, and optional tremolos, which the Les Paul rarely has.

Many other companies now produce variations with their own modifications, but the initial designs still stem from the 1950s design of Fender and Gibson. What has never changed is the sound of the instruments and the individuality that their pickups and construction differences allow. Both designs are as popular today as they were upon their introduction.

Acoustic Guitars

Acoustic guitars fall into two families: steel string and nylon string. Steel-string guitars are favored by folk and country players, while nylon-string guitars are traditionally used by classical players. When people speak of acoustic guitar, chances are they're talking about a steel-string acoustic. Some of the important names in acoustic guitar manufacturing are Martin, Taylor, Ovation, Gibson, and Fender.

Since these guitars don't rely on electronics, the only tonal differences you'll find among them are in the woods used to construct them. Currently, many acoustics are available with an optional electric pickup to help amplify the sound. Even if you don't plan on playing with an amp, it's a good idea to have a pickup on your guitar. Many sound technicians prefer to use the internal pickups rather than place a microphone in front of an acoustic guitar for sound reinforcement.

Amplifiers

For guitarists, the amplifier is an instrument all by itself, because it tends to color the original sound of the guitar, rather than just reproduce a louder signal. Because of this, amplifiers have a great deal to do with the sound of your guitar. Amps fall into two categories: tube and solid state. There are two dominant amp manufacturers: Fender and Marshall.

Tube Amps

Tube amps are the most common amplifiers in use. They're called "tube amps" because they use vacuum tube technology to generate power and distortion. Tube amps fall into two categories: American and British. The American amps, made by Fender, have a long tradition of being "clean" amps, because they produce a clean and loud signal without much distortion. Their sound is legendary, and as a result, vintage Fender amps command serious prices when sold. In the old days, distortion was seen as a bad thing and amp manufacturers went out of their way to prevent it. As time progressed, distortion became a permanent part of rock guitar sound, although it was discovered more or less by accident. The Fender Twin is one of the most famous amp designs and embodies the American sound: strident and clean. You could turn these amps up very loud without any sound deterioration or unwanted distortion (yes, there was a time when distortion was bad!).

FACT

Even though the vacuum tube has been replaced in our society by smaller transistors, tube amps have a legendary tone that players don't want to give up. Because of this, the tube market has stayed around, although much smaller than it was forty years ago, just for guitarists and other audiophiles who love the warm sound of tubes.

Marshall Amplifiers, manufactured in England, differ greatly from their Fender counterparts. The amps, while clean at low volumes, tend to distort greatly when turned up. The louder they're played, the more distorted they become. This is one of the reasons that rock and roll music was always so loud—players had to crank their amps all the way up to get the desired tone. Marshall Amps became famous for their distorted sound and became the alternative to the Fender sound. Fender amps did distort slightly when turned all the way up, but not to the extent that Marshalls did.

As time progressed, other amp manufacturers began to enter the amp market basing their designs on pre-existing Marshall and Fender designs. Mesa Boogie began their amplifier line by modifying old Fender Princeton amps and adding more gain and power to them. Mesa Boogie became successful with their first amp, the Mark I, and is now a legend in the amplifier world. Some of the other big names in amps are: Crate, Vox, Carvin, Ampeg, Peavey, and Matchless.

Solid State

Tubes were replaced by smaller and more durable integrated circuits in the 1960s. One of the main drawbacks to tube amps is that tubes wear out over time, and most amps don't sound good unless cranked to 10. Solid state amps don't use tubes, and they're smaller and lighter than tube amps. The majority of amps, especially in the beginners market, are solid state. Solid state amps are more durable and dependable than tube amps, and over their lifetime require little or no service, but they've long been criticized for lacking some of the warmth of tube amps. However, some players are fond of the sound that solid state amps make and make them part of their sound. Either way you slice it, it's a matter of personal taste. In the low end of the amp market, you won't find many tube amps under $500, or many solid state amps over $500.

Combos vs. Stacks

Many amps come as all-in-one units, called "combo amps," because they combine the speaker and the amp into one unit. Larger amps are available with separate heads and speakers that you can combine. Of course, you've all seen those impressive eight-foot-tall full stacks at the music store. While stack amps look great, and are great for your ego, they tend to be very bulky and hard to transport. The only advantage they have is sheer volume, because they're built to play much louder than the combo amps are. In reality, you'll never need to play that loud. Most venues have P.A. systems, so you'll be able to mike your amp through the house system. This will allow you to play at a comfortable volume level onstage, while the soundman takes care of the rest. For most players, combo amps are easier to deal with because they are smaller and lighter.

How Loud?

How loud do you need to be? Most amps are rated in watts, and for most professional players, 50 watts is plenty, but 100 watts is preferred. But the watt rating can be deceiving because different amps have different volumes. You can tell a lot from the speaker size. Most amps with smaller speakers are not suitable for loud playing. You should look for a ten-inch speaker, at the minimum. However, on bigger amps you'll find twelve-inch speakers are more common.

Digital Amps

Technology has changed our lives, and for guitar players it has changed our sound. One of the drawbacks of solid-state amps is that they sound sterile compared to their tube counterparts. Digital modeling, via computers, has enabled amp designers to model the way a tube reacts in computer software. This technology has grown tremendously in the last few years. It seems that everyone is getting on the bandwagon, although the pioneer in this field is Line6.

Digital amps allow you to choose what you want to hear. You can change from a Fender twin, to a Marshall plexi with the touch of a button. Most digital amps include many different amps modeled after the legendary amps of rock and roll. As the technology keeps improving, the quality of the sounds also keeps improving. You can fool even the most ardent tube purist! Many players prefer digital amps and view them as the "Swiss army knives" of amplifiers.

For many players, this digital technology has allowed them to use only one amp, when in the past they would tour with many different amps for different tones. These digital amps also include built-in effects like reverb, delay, chorus, and many other standard effects. Many companies make digital amps, most notably Fender, Line6, Crate, Digitech, and Johnson.

Distortion

Distortion comes in many flavors, but the mechanics behind distortion is always the same. Distortion is the intentional overloading of a signal. If you've ever turned your stereo too loud and heard a crackling noise, you've experienced distortion. Distortion can be achieved by turning your amp up too loud and getting natural distortion, or you can use an effect pedal that will simulate the effect at lower volumes. Distortion comes in so many different types, that it is hard to explain how one is different from another.

Effects commonly come in two varieties: single pedals and rack units. The single pedals are self-contained units that usually have one effect. Rack units are digital processors that are programmable and contain many different effects that can be chained together. Racks were very popular in the 1980s, and while they're still in favor with touring professionals, most players prefer the convenience of single pedals. Single pedals are also much less expensive, running an average of $50.

Like amps, each pedal has its own character. What varies from effect to effect is the amount of distortion you can dial in and the amounts of control you have to power the sound. Some pedals, like those in the Tubeworks line, actually include a real pre-amp tube for distortion. Overdrive pedals specialize in low amounts of distortion and are favored by blues players who prefer adding only a little dirt to their sound. Overdrive pedals are typically used in conjunction with tube amps to improve the tone. A famous overdrive pedal is the Ibanez TS-9 Tubescreamer, used by just about everybody.

Distortion pedals are the harsher pedals and are used commonly in rock and heavy metal. These pedals dial in a lot of gain. If you're looking for a sound reminiscent of Metallica and Pantera, you'll need a distortion pedal. Listen to a variety of pedals and find the one that suits you the best.

Delay, Chorus, Reverb, and Flange

Delay is a standard effect that many players use. It's a simple effect that takes your original guitar tone and duplicates it, sending it back through the amp at a later time. The effect gives you the feeling of playing in an echo chamber. If the delay is quick, it can be used to fatten up a guitar tone.

One of the most creative uses of delay is by U2's the Edge. The Edge uses delay in a unique way; he sets the delay very fast with many repeats and when he plucks one note, you hear four or five successive ones. Delay, when used, is not always noticeable, but it can have a dramatic effect on your sound.

Chorus is an effect that takes your original signal, makes a copy of it, slightly detunes it, and sends it to the amp mixed with your original signal. The effect sounds as if more than one player is playing, and the detuning is to approximate the sound of two players who are never perfectly in tune. Chorus is a standard effect on clean guitar sounds and can be applied to distorted sounds as well.

FACT

The market has recently seen the introduction of multi-effect floor units. These units usually contain reverb, distortion, delay, and chorus, and, like racks, can be configured in many custom setups. Many of these units have pedals to switch effects on and off. Most of all, these multi-effects floor units are convenient and easy to carry, unlike racks, which require heavy rack carriers, and unlike single pedals that eat batteries and require many small patch cables. Multi-effect floor units are made by Boss, Roland, Korg, Line6, Behringer, Digitech, and others.

Reverb tries to duplicate the natural echo of playing in a large hall, giving the effect of distance and aural space to your sound. Reverb is a subtle effect and can really improve your standard guitar tone; in spite of that, don't use too much of it because it can obscure your sound. Most amps come with onboard reverb, but some players like to have more control, so they opt for outboard gear.

Flange is an effect that sounds like a jet plane swooshing overhead, and duplicates the old recording trick of touching the flange head on a tape recording machine. Soundgarden used flange on "Black Hole Sun."

The Wah

The wah, or wah-wah, is an effect achieved with a pedal called an "envelope shifter." The pedal works like a super tone knob and dramatically changes your tone from dark to light. The change is initiated from the player's foot rocking back and forth. The most popular pedals are made by Dunlop and Vox, although there are others made by such companies as Morley or Boss. The name "wah" comes from the sound made when you rock your foot back and forth. You'll have to hear it to really understand the sound. Hendrix popularized this pedal, and it has become a staple of guitar players everywhere.

Chapter 19

Technology

Changes in technology in the past fifty years have had a huge impact on guitar-playing. Electric guitar players have been riding a wave of progress that shows no signs of stopping. In the last few years, the dawn of digital amp modeling has revolutionized the sounds players can create. In general, the computer has opened up doors to musicians that have changed the way we work and play.

Early Synthesizers

Early synthesizers created sound by turning electrical voltage into sound. Through the use of electrical filters (just like the knobs on your guitar and amp), the sound could be shaped into different waves and different sounds. Keyboard instruments were the first instruments to be used as synth controllers because of the simplicity of the instrument's layout. Every note has its own key, and it was easy for early designers to associate a note with a particular voltage. While synthesizers weren't able to recreate the sound of a piano, they could create sounds you couldn't get anywhere else. If you like Pink Floyd, ELP, and Yes, you've heard these keyboard synths.

The original style of synthesizing was called analog synthesis because it relied on analog voltage to make the sound. As technology progressed, keyboards became digitally controlled. Gone were the days of filters and voltages; now keyboards could trigger samples that were interpreted by a computer. Samples are pieces of music played on real instruments that have been digitally recorded and played back using keyboard-style instruments. Each keyboard had its own system and programming language that it worked with. Because each one was different, it was impossible for keyboards to work together with computers—each spoke a different language.

While each keyboard spoke a different language, the information it passed was remarkably similar. Each keyboard had to define certain events: note on, note off, and how loud. Simply, that's all there was to making a note on a digital keyboard—on, off, and volume. Because each keyboard was essentially trying to say the same thing, the standard language of MIDI was created to allow keyboards and computers to work together.

MIDI

The first major technological shift came with the invention of the Musical Instrument Digital Interface, or MIDI for short. MIDI was, and still is, a way for musical instruments to communicate via computers, and it set a standard language for musical performance control. The world of MIDI is predominantly for keyboard-style instruments, but alternate instruments have been explored.

FACT

Player pianos read long sheets of paper with perforations punched out that correspond to pitches, and the piano interprets that information into music with automated key presses. In the computer age, the long rolls of paper are replaced by programming and computer control.

MIDI is simply a computer language that controls the playing of a musical instrument. Since the keyboard is just sending messages saying what note to play, when to stop, and how loud to play it, there is now the possibility of letting the computer do the same work by transmitting the information directly into the keyboard. Not only is MIDI a language, it is also a hardware connection, via a five-pin connection that allows all computers and MIDI-capable instruments to connect universally, much like the universal serial bus (USB) does for modern computers.

Once computers were able to control synthesized sounds, prerecording and editing became possible. Now, in combination with a computer, you can slowly play a difficult part from the keyboard and have the computer record your movements. After you are done playing the part, you can go back and fix mistakes, change tempos, and change pitches. It's now possible to use the computer as a recording and editing controller, and then have it play back the sounds through the synthesizer, at any speed. Lavish multipart orchestrations by one performer are now possible because the performer can simply push a button and have the computer play back twenty or more tracks at once.

The Guitar's Role

Keyboard players were having a lot of fun, especially in the early 1980s, with the invention of MIDI. Because all synths used the keyboard-style interface, piano players were able to unlock the world of computer music, while other instruments were left in the dust. This is not to say that guitar was left out of the synth game altogether. In the early days of analog synth, there were many successful guitar synths.

The first guitar synths started to enter the market in the late 1970s. Because of how analog synthesis works, the guitar was a good candidate to act as a synth controller. The string's vibration could easily be converted to voltage and sent through the synth engine. Early guitar synths were marketed by Roland and ARP. These guitars had a vast array of sounds, but few musicians really unlocked their secrets. The most successful analog guitar synth playing came from Pat Metheny, Adrian Belew (King Crimson), and Andy Summers (The Police). The guitar was very successful as a synth controller, but the advent of MIDI complicated life for the guitar player.

Complications

There are two factors that make a keyboard-style instrument a good synth controller: (1) The keyboard makes it very easy for the synth to determine what note you're playing, because each key has its own sensor, and a computer easily deciphers its messages; and (2) keyboard notes are either on or off and rarely have much nuance. Because of these factors, the keyboard has been the most successful of all MIDI controller instruments. When the synthesizers relied on pitch to voltage, the guitar did a nice job because that's what normal electric guitars do— they transfer the string's vibration to an electric charge via the magnetic pickups. When MIDI took over, things got very complicated for guitarists.

In order to detect what note you were playing, the guitar synth units had to analyze the waveform you played to detect a pitch. It took at least two full cycles through the waveform to detect pitch. On a keyboard, analysis could be done instantaneously, but on guitar synths it was delayed. Because of the differences in pitch on the guitar, lower strings took longer to play than higher ones due to differences in pitch and frequency. While the delay was measured in milliseconds, it spelled big trouble for guitar players. You played a note and the unit took awhile to catch up.

Guitar is an instrument filled with expression and nuance. Slides, vibrato, and bends further confused early MIDI guitars and caused headaches for the players. With technological advances, guitar synth has improved, but the technology still relies on figuring out what you're playing and converting it to MIDI data. And no matter how fast the machine is, there's still a delay—although it's much better now. While computers have gotten faster, the delay is still present. Present-day units are very useable, but don't expect them to respond exactly like a guitar. To this day, Roland, one of the first guitar-synth makers, has been producing guitar synths since the late 1970s. Other companies that manufacture synths are Yamaha, Axon, and Shadow. Modern guitar synths attach to your guitar with a small hex pickup that senses the sound and feeds it to the synth box for translation.

ALERT!

Forget about string bends—early MIDI units couldn't handle them. To get MIDI to work, you either had to play very slowly or have the cleanest technique ever, with no bends or slides to confuse the unit. Because of these quirks and difficulties, guitar synths have never really caught on, unlike the keyboard-style synths.

Workable Synths

The current MIDI technology for use with guitars has its limitations; if you've ever tried to rip a fast line on a guitar synth, you may remember feeling slightly displaced as the unit couldn't quite keep up. Several attempts have been made to approach the problem from a different angle. The two synths that have utilized different technology are the Synthaxe and the Ztar.

The Synthaxe was introduced in 1984 and was the brainchild of British designer Bill Aitken. What made the Synthaxe so different was that instead of relying on MIDI to analyze pitch, the fingerboard was wired to detect where you were playing. The strings on the fingerboard were dummy strings and made no sound; they only aided in making the guitar player feel at home on the neck. The dummy strings also detected pitch bend and vibrato information. Because the neck could sense where you were, there was no lag or delay in the process of playing; you could play quite fast. There was a second set of strings on the body that you could pick, and these strings sensed your volume. There were also buttons for triggering strings and samples from the body of the instrument, and a breath controller for blowing note volumes with breath. One catch: this perfect MIDI system capable of controlling any MIDI sound source or computer cost about $20,000!

With the invention of the Synthaxe, guitar players for the first time could play with guitar technique and make the sound of a trumpet come out, or piano, or whatever you wanted. Interaction with the computer was near perfect, too, but the price tag puts it largely out of reach for most players. Its most notable player is Allan Holdsworth, who plays so fast and clean on it you won't believe what you're hearing. The company went under and there are few left in the world.

In 1992, Starr Labs of San Diego, California, designed the Ztar, a unique guitar synthesizer controller. The Synthaxe fingerboard system worked well, but had many small parts and was hard to service and maintain. The Ztar set out to emulate the only true MIDI controller: the keyboard. Instead of strings, the fingerboard is laid out with pressure sensitive keys just like a piano—one key for each fret (6 x 24 = 144 keys) and each key is responsible for one note. There are no delays with this system, and no strings either. Since the buttons are small raised keys, they emulate the feeling of strings, so the dummy strings aren't necessary.

Unlike other guitar synths the Ztar can play multiple notes per "string," something no real stringed instrument can ever do. This makes two-handed playing on the fingerboard an accessible technique.

On the body, the Ztar has an impressive number of options for playing, with either trigger bars or real strings for picking. Breath control is an option; joystick and computer readout is standard. The Ztar plugs into any MIDI interface, sound module, or computer via a standard five-pin MIDI cable. The Ztar is still produced today in several models and options, and remains the most drastic alternative to the current pitch-to-MIDI solutions on the market. The Ztar is, most notably, used by Stanley Jordan. I used the Ztar, myself, to compose the examples in this book and notate them on the computer via Sibelius notation software.

Guitar Synth Uses

As a live performance tool, a guitar synth can enable you to unlock sounds never before possible. You can play a string orchestra behind a soft ballad, and a piano part is now possible even if you don't have a keyboard player in the band. You can use it for an expressive lead sound (à la Pat Metheny), or it can be a great tool for composing music. With the aid of a computer, a guitar synth is the ultimate link between the computer world and the guitar world. Without guitar synth, you would have a hard time utilizing the exciting world of MIDI and computer music.

Sequencers

A sequencer is a piece of software that records the MIDI events onto a computer and then lets you manipulate them onscreen. This is called sequencing and is one of the most popular uses of MIDI. Think of a sequencer as a tape recorder for MIDI, but unlike a tape recorder, you can have virtually unlimited tracks.

The amount of control you have while editing is unparalleled. If you're interested in recording home demos, being able to sequence a background string part, flute line, or piano line to play over is invaluable. Many professional musicians prepare fully working demos of their music this way, before presenting it to other band members. If you don't have a guitar synth, don't worry. Most sequencing programs let you enter notes into a notation window for constructing various instrumental parts; using a guitar synth or a keyboard controller is just a much faster way for note entry. Once the tracks are into the computer, you can tweak individual notes, change keys and tempos, add effects, and even fix rhythmic mistakes.

MIDI files are small and you can fit many files on your computer, even with a small hard disk. Some bands use sequenced parts live and play them through a laptop computer. The most popular sequencers are Cubase, Logic, Vision, and Cakewalk. Sequencing is a great tool because it gives you total control over the instruments and their sound. If you don't have musicians near you to play with, sequencing can be a great tool for music creation and composing.

In the old days, Apple Macintosh computers were exclusively used for music and audio. In the last few years, the Microsoft Windows operating system has been adopted by musicians and recording engineers. Today, whatever you would like to do on a computer, you can do it equally on either machine. Traditionally, you will see more Macintoshes than PCs in recording studios, but that's changing. Talk to other musicians and try out both the Mac OS and Windows before making a big purchase.

Notation

Another popular use for MIDI is in music notation software. Just as word processors have made handwriting less common, music notation software is making old-fashioned pencil-and-paper composing less common. Notation programs not only print out neater and more professional looking music than you could do by hand, they also alleviate some of the torture work of composing music. The two most prominent software notation tools are Finale and Sibelius. Finale has been around longer and is the standard, but Sibelius is gaining ground and popularity with composers. Both do the same task of creating printed music.

Both programs are MIDI capable, meaning that you can play something on a keyboard or guitar synth, MIDI will analyze it, and the program will notate it onscreen. You can then simply click and drag your music and make it tablature, transpose it for other instruments, or orchestrate parts for large ensembles. Transposing music for other instruments has long been the bane of music students; via software, transposing is done automatically. If you plan to teach music, or write for other musicians, notation software is a must.

For a great example of computers and music working together, look at any of the music examples in this book. All the music examples were played into a PC using a Ztar MIDI synth guitar directly into Sibelius notation software and converted to tablature instantly. Using both of these tools, the music creation was done at a rapid rate, almost like speaking into a word processor.

Home Recording

The world of home recording has exploded in the last ten years. Before then, home recording was the luxury of the few rich musicians who could afford all the gear, tape machines, and studio consoles necessary to produce music in their homes. With the never-ending increases of computer speed, the recording studio has become a "virtual studio" living inside a computer. With some extra hardware to handle audio inputs and outputs, a relatively powerful machine can become a full-fledged audio workstation.

It is now possible for a home/hobby musician to get results that sound as clean and professional as most studios, and burn the finished CD at home. If you don't own a computer, there are also small portable recording units made by Roland, Akai, and Boss that function as stand-alone recording studios. They include effects and editing, and now some have built-in CD burners. While portable studios work, computer studios offer some distinct advantages.

Editing Capabilities of Home Computers

Home computers have the benefit of being able to do better editing than portable studios can do. With a monitor, mouse, and keyboard, most of the editing can be done simply. If you record a guitar part that you'd like to repeat at the end, you can copy or drag it to the new location, just as you copy and paste in a word processor. Editing can be done in precise ways, and punch-ins can be controlled with great precision.

Most recording software also has onboard MIDI sequencing so you can mix MIDI tracks and real audio tracks for the ultimate home studio setup. Popular audio recording software is: Ensoniq Paris, Digidesign Pro Tools, Logic Audio, and Steinberg Cubase VST. In the professional recording world, Pro Tools reigns as the standard, and most mid-size and large studios rely on Pro Tools systems, too.

Many of your favorite albums have been recorded directly by computers. Computers have many advantages over traditional recording systems. Ease of editing is just one of the features. Computers allow you to have greater control over the audio and allow tweaks of performance. Say you recorded five takes of a song. The bass player sounds the best on take two, but your solo was better on take four. On a computer, the individual takes can be combined into a "super take" with little effort. On a traditional tape system this would be impossible.

Software Plug-Ins

Computers also let you create amazing effects via software. With no more expensive racks, the computer software effects are software plug-ins that reproduce reverb and other popular effects. Some of these effects can automatically tune the "out of tune" vocals and emulate the sound of old tape recordings. The most important factor for the home studio owner is the price/performance ratio. With a decent computer and minimal purchases of software and hardware, you can create great-sounding demos at home from the start to the final CD creation. No more hourly studio rates—you can work when you want to! Many artists, including famous ones, are investing in home studios and recording albums with little expense, thus saving tremendous amounts of money.

Other Uses for the Home Computer

Besides music creation, the computer helps in so many different ways. You can use a spreadsheet to plot your practice time. You can create great-looking pages to promote your band. You can burn your own CDs at home and sell them at your gigs.

A popular piece of guitar software is a chord program that contains hundreds of chords in a database format. There are also shareware metronomes and scale learning programs. If you can think of it, chances are that someone has created software to help it. There is even software available on the Internet to help you learn guitar. If you have programming chops, you can create your own software to help your study skills. Teachers now give lessons via e-mail, making distance learning with professional musicians possible. Explore the Web to see what's out there. Look in Appendix A for some useful links.

Many students are excited at the amount of free tablature available online. It's possible to search for your favorite song and quickly find a text file containing the guitar parts. However, Internet tab is illegal, for starters, and more importantly it is grossly inaccurate. Tab like this is written by other students and is wrought with inaccuracies of chords and fingerings. While it may be convenient, you're much better off buying books from a music store for this. Not only are they professionally prepared and correctly written out, but you also help pay the musicians for their work.

Chapter 20
The Next Steps

Now that you've gotten this far, you may be wondering, what's next? The answer is, you need to take steps to ensure that you continue to grow and learn. In this chapter you will find tips for lifelong success and enjoyment of music.

Finish Line

You've come a long way, so pat yourself on the back. In the preceding chapters you learned the basics of music and applied them to rock and blues music; but these basics apply to all styles. If you decide to study jazz at some point, you can use the same scales and arpeggios appearing in this book, except in a different way. The basic information stays the same. In a way, you've learned more than you think.

However, just reading the material in this book and playing some of the examples doesn't mean that you know it. Learning a scale position doesn't mean that you understand a scale. The difference between superficial learning and true knowledge is important to understand. So, if you just skimmed this book, go back and reread it and practice some more. Learning music to a level where you can create it is a deep and mysterious task that can't be rushed. It's like learning to speak your native language—sure you picked up small words and phrases early, but it took many years to speak fluently. The same holds true for music. If you really want to learn, the material in this book can last you a lifetime.

The Path

Boston guitar teacher Jon Finn speaks about "The Path" and finding your own way. Use the basic building blocks of music—scales, intervals, and chords—and work hard to find your own way as a musician. When you practice, try to find new and inventive ways to play the instrument. Find a new way to play a scale. In the beginning, study great players, but don't take what they do as gospel. The truly great players are all innovators in some way. Their inventiveness is what made them so great, not how much they sounded like someone else.

It's very easy to use clichés when playing guitar. If you've spent time learning licks, it's easy for you to stay there forever and not change how you play. But once you learn the basic tools of guitar playing, you should take those tools and seek out your own path to create your own music. For example, if you give three graphic artists the same pencil and paper, you'll get three different drawings. Same tools—different outcomes. The same thing holds true in music: Give three guitar players the same notes, scales, and chords, and each musician will create different music. The great artists transcend the instrument and use it as a tool, not just a guitar.

FACT

Try this experiment: Get an old guitar and buy a whole bunch of small stickers from a crafts store. Place the stickers under the strings according to a scale diagram (there are plenty in Chapter 6). This will highlight the correct notes and leave the wrong notes empty. Now play. Notice that, since you have the whole neck available to you, you tend to use all of the notes. In general, after practicing this way, most players find themselves playing all over the neck and rarely, if ever, go back to scale boxes. The scale box patterns are convenient because they help you learn three or four frets at a time, but the fret stickers allow you to explore freely.

Building Blocks

Not learning *all* the notes on the fret board is the most significant obstacle to understanding how to play the guitar. Knowing what notes are in an A-minor arpeggio is fine and dandy, but if you don't know how to find those on the neck, it's just wasted information. Once you understand all the notes on the neck, everything opens up. Even if you love the way you play right now, learn all the notes on the neck anyway.

Start every day with a review of the notes A, B, C, D, E, F, and G on every string. In time you will learn them better and be able to use them more easily. Once you know what the name of the note is, you'll be more apt to analyze what you're doing. For example, why does the twelfth fret on the first string sound so good on an E blues? Because that note is an E, which is the keynote (which always sounds good). You may notice you're playing certain frets over and over again. How do those frets relate to the chord you're playing on? If you're not fret-board literate, you're flying blind. That's one of the reasons players don't achieve the potential of their guitar playing—they're blocked by what they don't know. So get in the know!

Approach the Guitar Another Way

Moveable shapes make the guitar easy to learn to play, and no other instrument can be learned this way. When a sax player wants to learn a scale, he or she learns what notes make up that scale and applies it to the fingerings on the instrument. Since every scale has different notes and different fingerings, sax players don't have the convenience of moveable shapes.

But moveable shapes can also inhibit learning on the guitar. In the early stages, guitar students get a certain amount of freedom using them. The ability to play in all twelve keys from the beginning is a huge advantage. While guitar players are jamming away mindlessly, the other instrumentalists are learning key by key what to play and what sounds good based on note names, not just fingerings. Guitar players tend to learn fingerings and forget about notes, so they never learn every note on the neck of their instrument. Not knowing the neck doesn't prevent you from playing in the early stages, but it will catch up with you later.

There is a real sense of liberation when you can play without having to think about it. But beware: Once you become a better player, you may find yourself locked into patterns, always playing the same thing. This is a natural byproduct of shape learning. Your ears and brain equate certain repeating finger movements with sounds, and you get stuck in licks. To break out of this, it's sometimes helpful to go back and study the guitar the way students of other instruments study theirs.

The piano is a wonderful instrument. If you know how the keyboard is set up, you can look down and easily name any note on the instrument with ease. Try that on the guitar! The piano is a visual instrument laid out in a straight line; its relationships and intervals are very easy to see. Remember in Chapter 7 where you learned scale shapes across one single string—no box shapes, no position, just pure notes in a straight line? This is very reminiscent of the piano.

The piano also has black and white keys, which make seeing the notes very easy. The guitar has just strings and frets, and they all look the same! The ability to see the guitar like a piano is very difficult and requires tremendous discipline. Is it really that hard? No. At first you may be flustered, because this will put you back to being a beginner player, but after a while it will start to make sense and you'll "get it." The good news is that there are only twelve keys, and in reality only a few of them are used.

You'll be amazed at how looking at the guitar this way changes your playing. When you eliminate patterns and shapes, you will immediately stop the mindless licks and become more focused on playing musically. By removing these conveniences you'll start to think about music in a purer way. In time you will establish your own vocabulary that you can start to learn all over the neck. Eventually you will again find uses for the positions and scale shapes, but now you will see the guitar as a whole. Using shapes is fine, as long as it isn't the only way you play. You can take this many steps further by studying how other instruments work and trying to incorporate that knowledge into your playing.

Get Good Instruction

Get a good teacher who can simplify material and present it in a logical order tailored to your progress. This book can't tailor a program for you, but your teacher can use this material and help you apply it. A good teacher can unlock the secrets of music and change your life. Most teachers are also performers and will have lots of experience playing the guitar in many different situations. If you can't find a good teacher near you, find other players whom you admire and hang out with them. You'll pick up so much just by watching and playing along, which is also why you can learn a lot from guitar videos. Whether they're instructional or live concert videos, you can learn a great deal just from studying players' fingers.

Keep Learning

At the beginning of any new process, learning happens at an accelerated pace. Every day you seem to learn something new. As you progress, you'll find that your playing becomes harder and harder to improve. Ruts last longer, and progress seems more drawn out. This is normal, and oddly enough, is a good sign. The better you are, the harder it is to improve. It's harder because you know more, and the new elements become more and more advanced.

The good news is that there is no end to how much music you can create and study. If you feel you're in a particularly bad rut, try playing jazz, classical, or country guitar for a change of pace. Many great players have studied other styles of guitar playing and incorporated them into their style.

QUESTION?

How much do I have to know?
Learn everything you can get your hands on, even if you can't see a reason for it or a need at the present moment. Just like carrying emergency money hidden in your wallet may seem silly, when you need it you'll be glad you have it. As you learn more, your playing will change. Learn it all and then decide what you want to use. There is no such thing as useless information. Let it lay dormant until you need it.

Listen Freely

To be a well-informed musician, you need to have an open mind. It's so important to listen to music other than rock and blues. While Stevie Ray Vaughan may be the reason you picked up guitar, you will find inspiration from other styles of music, too. If you're trying to write a beautiful melody, check out classical music, because it's packed full of beautiful melodies. While classical instrumentation is different, the basic structure is the same—it's just chords, scales, and melodies. Many fine players have been influenced by diverse music. For example, The Beatles were into the music of India, which has provided inspiration for a lot of players. Many players appreciate jazz because it is so rooted in the blues. If you can inject diverse influences into your own music, you may find interesting results.

Learn Everything

Most of us like to learn by doing. Examples in this book seemed more real after you heard them on the CD and played them yourself. If you want to learn about how to play the instrument, everyone should get a solid foundation in the "classics." The amount of information you can learn by playing someone else's material is immeasurable. You'll find it to be a common thread among good players; intimate knowledge of great guitarists and their work. Think of it like an apprenticeship; you study with a master and after a while you have honed your skills enough to go out and make your own decisions. If you like a certain player a lot and you feel that they epitomize the way you wish to play, emulate them. Learn every solo, every song. Dissect it and figure out how it works.

Don't Be Scared to Copy

I've touched on this before and want to emphasize how important it is to learn from other people's works. Unfortunately, there is a movement of people who believe that studying someone else's work closely will harm your own personal growth. This is simply untrue. Music doesn't exist in a vacuum. This is especially true in the genre of rock and blues music where there is a lineage that has been passed down.

What you should be careful of is lacking vision. Study players and learn how music works through them. After you feel confident, go off on your own and seek your own truth. Leave the master and become your own master. All the greats downright stole from their heroes. There is nothing wrong with that as long as you use it as a learning experience and not as the gospel of how to play guitar.

Get Out of Your Comfort Zone

One of the quickest ways to improve is to put yourself in a situation where you have to rely on your weak points. For example if you're a bad sight-reader, join a community jazz band and try to read a chart. Sure, you'll sound terrible the first night, but being in that situation will force you to learn how to read a chart. It's the same experience many language students go through when they have to spend a week in a foreign country speaking the language—then it all comes together.

On-the-job training is crucial to improving your playing, and in the case of blues, is part of the learning tradition. You're expected to hang around clubs and sit in with other musicians and learn the ropes on stage. So if you find yourself excelling at home, go out and use what you know in real situations. Try as hard as you can to play with musicians who are much better than you. Sink or swim! Being around heavyweights will do wonders for your playing.

Songwriting

It's very difficult to talk about what makes a good song. Theory can explain why chords and scales work together but can't tell you if the song is any good. Like anything else, good songwriting takes practice. If you're into songwriting instead of soloing, you should try to compose a song every day, sometimes two. After you're done, write it down or record it and stuff it in a drawer for at least four weeks. After a month is up, go back and look over what you wrote. Over time, maybe out of the thirty or so tunes you wrote, you'll find five you like and one really good one. Just like practicing scales, songwriting takes persistence and hard work. You're probably not going to be very good at first, but after a while you'll get more comfortable with the process and you'll be more efficient.

Remember that music is an enjoyable thing. Don't feel as though you have to tackle this book all at once. There truly is a lifetime's worth of information here, so take your time. Study the parts that interest you and give the other ones a chance. Constantly revisit the old material to see how much you've learned and how differently you view it. Above all else, play the music that's in your heart and enjoy the richness that music offers. (E)

Appendices

Appendix A

Resources

Appendix B

Recommended Albums

Appendix C

Music Reading Tutorial

Appendix A

Resources

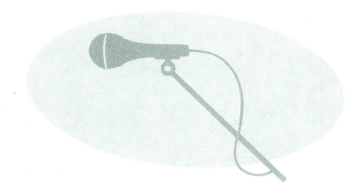

Books

Greene, Ted. *Modern Chord Progressions.* Miami, FL: Warner Brothers Publications, 1985.

Capuzzo, Guy. *Theory for the Contemporary Guitarist.* Van Nuys, CA: Alfred Publishing Co. 1996.

Goodrick, Mick. *The Advancing Guitarist.* Milwaukee, WI: Hal Leonard Publishing, 1987.

Green, Ted. *Chord Chemistry.* Miami, FL: Warner Brothers Publications, 1985.

Greene, Barry. *The Inner Game of Music.* Garden City, NY: Anchor Press/Doubleday, 1986.

Magazines

Acoustic Guitar—✐ *www.acousticguitar.com*
Guitar One—✐ *www.guitarmag.com*
Guitar World—✐ *www.guitarworld.com*
Just Jazz Guitar—✐ *www.justjazzguitar.com*

Videos

Albert Collins, Albert Collins, REH Video, 1992.
Blues and Beyond, Robben Ford, REH Video.
Blues Master, vols. 1, 2, and 3, B.B. King, DCI Video, 1991.
Electric Blues and Slide Guitar, Warren Haynes, Hot Licks.
The Fine Art of Guitar, Eric Johnson, Hot Licks.
Rock Discipline, John Petrucci, REH Video, 1996.

Web Sites

✐ *www.cdbaby.com*—Independent CD releases
✐ *www.guitar.com*—Online guitar guide
✐ *www.guitarsite.com*—Sites and songs
✐ *www.harmonycentral.com*—Links to guitar sites, info on gear, and online tabs
✐ *www.marcschonbrun.com*—The author's Web site
✐ *www.mp3.com*—A great place to find new players
✐ *www.slideguitar.com*—Slide instruction
✐ *www.musictheory.net*—Theory practice

Appendix B
Recommended Albums

Early Blues

Blind Lemon Jefferson, *Blind Lemon Jefferson*
Howlin' Wolf and Muddy Waters, *Muddy and the Wolf*
Robert Johnson, *King of the Delta Blues Singers*

Modern Blues

Albert Collins, *Frozen Alive*
Albert King, *Born under a Bad Sign*
B.B. King, *Live in Cook County Jail*
Stevie Ray Vaughan, *In Step*

Early Rock

Chuck Berry, *After School Session*
Buddy Holly, *Buddy Holly*
Jerry Lee Lewis, *Jerry Lee Lewis*
Elvis Presley, *Elvis' Golden Records*
Little Richard, *Here's Little Richard*

Classic Rock

AC/DC, *Highway to Hell*
The Beatles, *Let It Be* and *The White Album*
Jeff Beck, *Blow by Blow*
Eric Clapton, *The Cream of Clapton*
Pink Floyd, *Dark Side of the Moon* and *The Wall*
Jimi Hendrix, *Are You Experienced*
Led Zeppelin, *Led Zeppelin IV*
Rolling Stones, *Sticky Fingers*
The Who, *Tommy*

1980s and 1990s Rock

Metallica, *Metallica* and *Ride the Lightning*
Nirvana, *Nevermind*
Pearl Jam, *Ten*
Soundgarden, *Superunknown*
Stone Temple Pilots, *Core*
U2, *Achtung Baby*
Van Halen, *Van Halen*

Modern Rock

Dave Mathews Band, *Under the Table and Dreaming*
Green Day, *Dookie*
Incubus, *Science*
Korn, *Follow the Leader*
Radiohead, *O.K. Computer*
Red Hot Chili Peppers, *Californication*

Virtuoso Rock

Jason Becker, *Perpetual Burn*
Ritchie Blackmore, *Machine Head*
Paul Gilbert, *Street Legal*
Eric Johnson, *Ah Via Musicom*
Yngwie Malmsteen, *Rising Force*
Joe Satriani, *Surfing with the Alien*
Steve Vai, *Passion and Warfare*

Progressive Rock

Dream Theater, *Metropolis Part II: Scenes from a Memory*
Genesis, *Selling England by the Pound*
Kings X, *Gretchen Goes to Nebraska*
Rush, *Hemispheres* and *Moving Pictures*
Yes, *Yes Songs*

Jazz/Rock Fusion

Miles Davis, *In a Silent Way*
Al Di Meola, *Elegant Gypsy*
Scott Henderson, *Illicit*
Allan Holdsworth, *Metal Fatigue* and *The 16 Men of Tain*
John McLaughlin, *Mahavishnu Orchestra—Birds of Fire*
Pat Metheny, *Still Life Talking*

Acoustic Guitar/Finger Style

Michael Hedges, *Ariel Boundaries*
Leo Kottke, *Six & Twelve String Guitar*
Adrian Legg, *Guitar for Mortals*

Appendix C
Music Reading Tutorial

The music staff is made up of five lines and four spaces.

FIGURE C-1

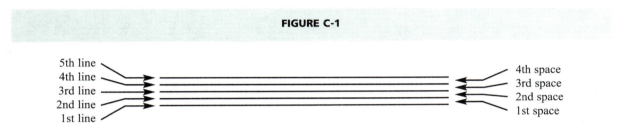

Notes can be placed either on the lines, or in the spaces. In music, the notes are named with the letters A through G; after G, A repeats. The G clef is the sign you see at the beginning of the line and indicates that the staff is in treble clef. Here are the notes on the G-clef staff.

FIGURE C-2

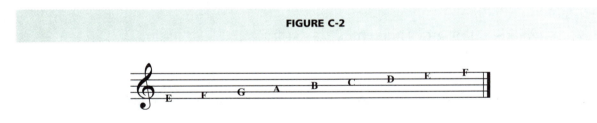

There's an easy way to remember what note goes where. For the lines, remember "Every Good Boy Does Fine"; for the spaces, remember the word "FACE."

FIGURE C-3

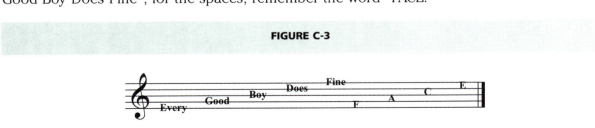

The staff can be separated by measures, which divide the music into smaller parts. Vertical measure lines break up the flow of the music and make it easier to read. At the end of a piece of music you will find a vertical double-bar line.

FIGURE C-4

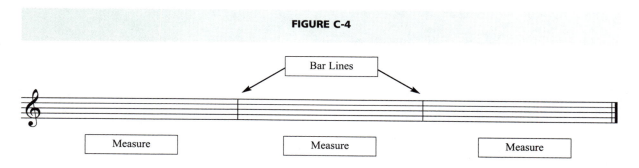

At the start of every piece of music you will see a time signature made up of two numbers. The time signature tells you how many beats to play in each measure and how to count them. The most commonly used time signature is 4/4. In music the time signature looks like a fraction without the line to divide it.

FIGURE C-5

The top number informs you how many counts per measure, and the bottom number tells you the type of note that gets counted. In 4/4 time, there are four counts to each measure, and the quarter note receives one count.

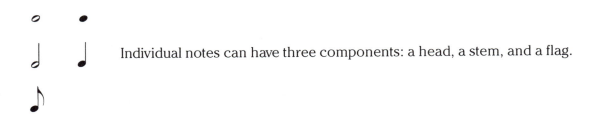

Individual notes can have three components: a head, a stem, and a flag.

Each note has a time value that can be determined by its appearance.

o This is a whole note, which gets four counts. In 4/4 time, you will see only one whole note per measure, or bar as it's also commonly called.

This is a half note, which gets two counts. You will see two of these in a 4/4 measure.

This is a quarter note, which gets one count. You will see four of these in a 4/4 measure.

This is an eighth note, which gets ½ of a count. You will see eight of these in a 4/4 measure.

This chart shows you how a single measure of 4/4 can be broken up.

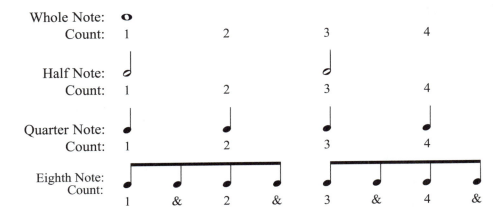

Index

A

A blues with turnaround chord, 182–183

A-Dorian, blues riffs and, 175, 176

A-Major scale with interval skips, 189

A-minor scale
added-ninth arpeggios, 122
arpeggio with hammer-ons, 158
bend/tap, 194–195

A-minor blues chord progression, 180, 181

A-minor blues scale, 61

A-minor hexatonic scale, 62–64

A-minor pentatonic scale, 26–28, 32
blues riffs and, 174–176
fingerboard diagrams, 54
hammer-ons and pull-offs, 50–51

pentatonic riff, 186
with slides, 40

A-Phrygian mode, in octaves, 192, 193

accessories, 233
amplifiers, 225–228
capos, 166
delay, chorus, reverb, and flange, 230–231
distortion and, 163, 229
EBow, 169
for home recording, 241–242
MIDI, 234–239, 242
for notation, 240
pick, 164–165
sequencers, 239–240
slides, 169–170
strings, 165
synthesizers, 234
wahs, 231

accidentals, 86–87

acoustic guitars, 225

added-ninth arpeggios, 122

Aeolian mode, 132

alternate tuning, 170–171

amplifiers, 225–228
combos versus stacks, 227–228
digital amps, 228
solid state amps, 227
tube amps, 226–227

arpeggios, 111
in blues progression, 123–124
fingerings for diminished, 118–119
fingerings for major, 114–116
fingerings for minor, 116–118
other than three-note, 121–122
practice tips for, 213, 216
in rock music, 192–196
sweep-picking and, 154–159
tapping of, 153–154
theory of, 112–114
uses of, 120–121

artificial harmonics, 168–169

reading charts of, 12–14
stable and unstable, 30–31
tapping of, 152–153
see also arpeggios
chorus, 230
chromatic notes, 86–87
chromatic tuner, 44–45
combo amplifiers, 227–228
computers, 242–243
    Apple versus Windows, 240
    author's use of, 241
    ear training and, 210
    home recording and,
        241–242
    MIDI and, 234–239
    notation and, 240–241
    sequencing with, 239–240

D

DADGAD tuning, 171
D-Dorian mode, 126–128
D-minor pentatonic scale, 187
    bend and release in, 47
    with taps, 193–194
D-minor scale, in thirds, 189
delay, 230
digital amplifiers, 228
diminished intervals, 86, 93
diminished triads, 100
distortion, 229
distortion filter, 163
dominant seventh chords,
    106
Dorian mode, 126–128, 134–135
    rock music and, 190–191

Dorian scale, 65
Drop-D tuning, 171
duration, of chord, 13–14

E

E blues, 182–183
E-diminished, arpeggio tapped,
    154
E-Dorian, 176, 177
E-Lydian mode, pedal point
    descending, 191
E-Major scale, 74
E-minor pentatonic scale,
    186–187
    blues riffs and, 176–177
    hammer-ons, 49
    pull-offs, 50
    with slides, 41
E-minor scale, 75–77, 196–197
    arpeggios, 192, 193
    pedal-point scale, 190
E-Mixolydian, 178, 179
E-Phrygian mode, 128–129
ear training, 168, 199
    advanced, 203–209
    beginning, 200–202
    computer help with, 210
    perfect versus relative pitch,
        200
    practice tips for, 213
    transcribing and, 209–210
EBow, 169
electric guitars, 4
    controlling sounds of,
        162–164

Fender style, 222–225
Gibson style, 222–225
hum from, 223
ending lines, blues and,
    181–183
enharmonic notes, 87–88, 90
envelope shifter, 231
extended chords, 102–109
    A blues with, 178, 179
    E blues with, 179, 180
    seventh chords, 103–106
    suspended chords, 106
extended techniques, 147
    sweep-picking, 154–159
    tapping, 148–154, 193–197

F

F-Lydian mode, 129–130
F-minor pentatonic scales,
    56–58
Fender, Leo, 222
Fender style guitars, 222–225
Fender Twin amplifier, 226
fifth chords, *see* power
    chords
fifths (intervals), ear training
    and, 206–207
fingers
    picking with, 165
    practice exercises, 143–146
    technique and, 140–143
flange, 231
flat notes, 86–87
forms, of pentatonic scale,
    55–59

THE EVERYTHING SERIES!

BUSINESS

Everything® **Business Planning Book**
Everything® **Coaching and Mentoring Book**
Everything® **Fundraising Book**
Everything® **Home-Based Business Book**
Everything® **Leadership Book**
Everything® **Managing People Book**
Everything® **Network Marketing Book**
Everything® **Online Business Book**
Everything® **Project Management Book**
Everything® **Selling Book**
Everything® **Start Your Own Business Book**
Everything® **Time Management Book**

COMPUTERS

Everything® **Build Your Own Home Page Book**
Everything® **Computer Book**
Everything® **Internet Book**
Everything® **Microsoft® Word 2000 Book**

COOKBOOKS

Everything® **Barbecue Cookbook**
Everything® **Bartender's Book, $9.95**
Everything® **Chinese Cookbook**
Everything® **Chocolate Cookbook**
Everything® **Cookbook**
Everything® **Dessert Cookbook**
Everything® **Diabetes Cookbook**
Everything® **Indian Cookbook**
Everything® **Low-Carb Cookbook**
Everything® **Low-Fat High-Flavor Cookbook**
Everything® **Low-Salt Cookbook**
Everything® **Mediterranean Cookbook**
Everything® **Mexican Cookbook**
Everything® **One-Pot Cookbook**
Everything® **Pasta Book**
Everything® **Quick Meals Cookbook**
Everything® **Slow Cooker Cookbook**
Everything® **Soup Cookbook**
Everything® **Thai Cookbook**
Everything® **Vegetarian Cookbook**
Everything® **Wine Book**

HEALTH

Everything® **Alzheimer's Book**
Everything® **Anti-Aging Book**
Everything® **Diabetes Book**
Everything® **Dieting Book**
Everything® **Herbal Remedies Book**
Everything® **Hypnosis Book**
Everything® **Massage Book**
Everything® **Menopause Book**
Everything® **Nutrition Book**
Everything® **Reflexology Book**
Everything® **Reiki Book**
Everything® **Stress Management Book**
Everything® **Vitamins, Minerals, and Nutritional Supplements Book**

HISTORY

Everything® **American Government Book**
Everything® **American History Book**
Everything® **Civil War Book**
Everything® **Irish History & Heritage Book**
Everything® **Mafia Book**
Everything® **Middle East Book**
Everything® **World War II Book**

HOBBIES & GAMES

Everything® **Bridge Book**
Everything® **Candlemaking Book**
Everything® **Casino Gambling Book**
Everything® **Chess Basics Book**
Everything® **Collectibles Book**
Everything® **Crossword and Puzzle Book**
Everything® **Digital Photography Book**
Everything® **Easy Crosswords Book**
Everything® **Family Tree Book**
Everything® **Games Book**
Everything® **Knitting Book**
Everything® **Magic Book**
Everything® **Motorcycle Book**
Everything® **Online Genealogy Book**
Everything® **Photography Book**
Everything® **Pool & Billiards Book**
Everything® **Quilting Book**
Everything® **Scrapbooking Book**
Everything® **Sewing Book**
Everything® **Soapmaking Book**

HOME IMPROVEMENT

Everything® **Feng Shui Book**
Everything® **Feng Shui Decluttering Book, $9.95 ($15.95 CAN)**
Everything® **Fix-It Book**
Everything® **Gardening Book**
Everything® **Homebuilding Book**

All Everything® books are priced at $12.95 or $14.95, unless otherwise stated. Prices subject to change without notice.
Canadian prices range from $11.95–$31.95, and are subject to change without notice.

Everything® **Home Decorating Book**
Everything® **Landscaping Book**
Everything® **Lawn Care Book**
Everything® **Organize Your Home Book**

EVERYTHING®
KIDS' BOOKS

All titles are $6.95
Everything® **Kids' Baseball Book,
3rd Ed.** ($10.95 CAN)
Everything® **Kids' Bible Trivia Book**
($10.95 CAN)
Everything® **Kids' Bugs Book** ($10.95 CAN)
Everything® **Kids' Christmas Puzzle &
Activity Book** ($10.95 CAN)
Everything® **Kids' Cookbook** ($10.95 CAN)
Everything® **Kids' Halloween Puzzle &
Activity Book** ($10.95 CAN)
Everything® **Kids' Joke Book** ($10.95 CAN)
Everything® **Kids' Math Puzzles Book**
($10.95 CAN)
Everything® **Kids' Mazes Book**
($10.95 CAN)
Everything® **Kids' Money Book**
($11.95 CAN)
Everything® **Kids' Monsters Book**
($10.95 CAN)
Everything® **Kids' Nature Book**
($11.95 CAN)
Everything® **Kids' Puzzle Book**
($10.95 CAN)
Everything® **Kids' Riddles & Brain
Teasers Book** ($10.95 CAN)
Everything® **Kids' Science Experiments
Book** ($10.95 CAN)
Everything® **Kids' Soccer Book**
($10.95 CAN)
Everything® **Kids' Travel Activity Book**
($10.95 CAN)

KIDS' STORY BOOKS

Everything® **Bedtime Story Book**
Everything® **Bible Stories Book**
Everything® **Fairy Tales Book**
Everything® **Mother Goose Book**

LANGUAGE

Everything® **Inglés Book**
Everything® **Learning French Book**
Everything® **Learning German Book**
Everything® **Learning Italian Book**
Everything® **Learning Latin Book**
Everything® **Learning Spanish Book**
Everything® **Sign Language Book**
Everything® **Spanish Phrase Book,**
$9.95 ($15.95 CAN)

MUSIC

Everything® **Drums Book (with CD),**
$19.95 ($31.95 CAN)
Everything® **Guitar Book**
Everything® **Playing Piano and
Keyboards Book**
Everything® **Rock & Blues Guitar
Book (with CD),** $19.95
($31.95 CAN)
Everything® **Songwriting Book**

NEW AGE

Everything® **Astrology Book**
Everything® **Divining the Future Book**
Everything® **Dreams Book**
Everything® **Ghost Book**
Everything® **Love Signs Book,** $9.95
($15.95 CAN)
Everything® **Meditation Book**
Everything® **Numerology Book**
Everything® **Palmistry Book**
Everything® **Psychic Book**
Everything® **Spells & Charms Book**
Everything® **Tarot Book**
Everything® **Wicca and Witchcraft Book**

PARENTING

Everything® **Baby Names Book**
Everything® **Baby Shower Book**
Everything® **Baby's First Food Book**
Everything® **Baby's First Year Book**
Everything® **Breastfeeding Book**

Everything® **Father-to-Be Book**
Everything® **Get Ready for Baby Book**
Everything® **Getting Pregnant Book**
Everything® **Homeschooling Book**
Everything® **Parent's Guide to
Children with Autism**
Everything® **Parent's Guide to Positive
Discipline**
Everything® **Parent's Guide to Raising
a Successful Child**
Everything® **Parenting a Teenager Book**
Everything® **Potty Training Book,**
$9.95 ($15.95 CAN)
Everything® **Pregnancy Book, 2nd Ed.**
Everything® **Pregnancy Fitness Book**
Everything® **Pregnancy Organizer,**
$15.00 ($22.95 CAN)
Everything® **Toddler Book**
Everything® **Tween Book**

PERSONAL FINANCE

Everything® **Budgeting Book**
Everything® **Get Out of Debt Book**
Everything® **Get Rich Book**
Everything® **Homebuying Book, 2nd Ed.**
Everything® **Homeselling Book**
Everything® **Investing Book**
Everything® **Money Book**
Everything® **Mutual Funds Book**
Everything® **Online Investing Book**
Everything® **Personal Finance Book**
Everything® **Personal Finance in Your
20s & 30s Book**
Everything® **Wills & Estate Planning
Book**

PETS

Everything® **Cat Book**
Everything® **Dog Book**
Everything® **Dog Training and Tricks
Book**
Everything® **Golden Retriever Book**
Everything® **Horse Book**
Everything® **Labrador Retriever Book**
Everything® **Puppy Book**
Everything® **Tropical Fish Book**

All Everything® books are priced at $12.95 or $14.95, unless otherwise stated. Prices subject to change without notice.
Canadian prices range from $11.95–$31.95, and are subject to change without notice.

REFERENCE

Everything® **Astronomy Book**
Everything® **Car Care Book**
Everything® **Christmas Book, $15.00**
    ($21.95 CAN)
Everything® **Classical Mythology Book**
Everything® **Einstein Book**
Everything® **Etiquette Book**
Everything® **Great Thinkers Book**
Everything® **Philosophy Book**
Everything® **Psychology Book**
Everything® **Shakespeare Book**
Everything® **Tall Tales, Legends, &**
    Other Outrageous
    Lies Book
Everything® **Toasts Book**
Everything® **Trivia Book**
Everything® **Weather Book**

RELIGION

Everything® **Angels Book**
Everything® **Bible Book**
Everything® **Buddhism Book**
Everything® **Catholicism Book**
Everything® **Christianity Book**
Everything® **Jewish History &**
    Heritage Book
Everything® **Judaism Book**
Everything® **Prayer Book**
Everything® **Saints Book**
Everything® **Understanding Islam**
    Book
Everything® **World's Religions Book**
Everything® **Zen Book**

SCHOOL & CAREERS

Everything® **After College Book**
Everything® **Alternative Careers Book**
Everything® **College Survival Book**
Everything® **Cover Letter Book**
Everything® **Get-a-Job Book**
Everything® **Hot Careers Book**

Everything® **Job Interview Book**
Everything® **New Teacher Book**
Everything® **Online Job Search Book**
Everything® **Resume Book, 2nd Ed.**
Everything® **Study Book**

SELF-HELP/ RELATIONSHIPS

Everything® **Dating Book**
Everything® **Divorce Book**
Everything® **Great Marriage Book**
Everything® **Great Sex Book**
Everything® **Kama Sutra Book**
Everything® **Romance Book**
Everything® **Self-Esteem Book**
Everything® **Success Book**

SPORTS & FITNESS

Everything® **Body Shaping Book**
Everything® **Fishing Book**
Everything® **Fly-Fishing Book**
Everything® **Golf Book**
Everything® **Golf Instruction Book**
Everything® **Knots Book**
Everything® **Pilates Book**
Everything® **Running Book**
Everything® **Sailing Book, 2nd Ed.**
Everything® **T'ai Chi and QiGong Book**
Everything® **Total Fitness Book**
Everything® **Weight Training Book**
Everything® **Yoga Book**

TRAVEL

Everything® **Family Guide to Hawaii**
Everything® **Guide to Las Vegas**
Everything® **Guide to New England**
Everything® **Guide to New York City**
Everything® **Guide to Washington D.C.**
Everything® **Travel Guide to The**
    Disneyland Resort®,
    California Adventure®,

Universal Studios®, and
the Anaheim Area
Everything® **Travel Guide to the Walt**
    Disney World Resort®,
    Universal Studios®, and
    Greater Orlando, 3rd Ed.

WEDDINGS

Everything® **Bachelorette Party Book,**
    $9.95 ($15.95 CAN)
Everything® **Bridesmaid Book, $9.95**
    ($15.95 CAN)
Everything® **Creative Wedding Ideas**
    Book
Everything® **Elopement Book, $9.95**
    ($15.95 CAN)
Everything® **Groom Book**
Everything® **Jewish Wedding Book**
Everything® **Wedding Book, 2nd Ed.**
Everything® **Wedding Checklist,**
    $7.95 ($11.95 CAN)
Everything® **Wedding Etiquette Book,**
    $7.95 ($11.95 CAN)
Everything® **Wedding Organizer,**
    $15.00 ($22.95 CAN)
Everything® **Wedding Shower Book,**
    $7.95 ($12.95 CAN)
Everything® **Wedding Vows Book,**
    $7.95 ($11.95 CAN)
Everything® **Weddings on a Budget**
    Book, $9.95 ($15.95 CAN)

WRITING

Everything® **Creative Writing Book**
Everything® **Get Published Book**
Everything® **Grammar and Style Book**
Everything® **Grant Writing Book**
Everything® **Guide to Writing**
    Children's Books
Everything® **Screenwriting Book**
Everything® **Writing Well Book**

Software License Agreement

YOU SHOULD CAREFULLY READ THE FOLLOWING TERMS AND CONDITIONS BEFORE USING THIS SOFTWARE PRODUCT. INSTALLING AND USING THIS PRODUCT INDICATES YOUR ACCEPTANCE OF THESE CONDITIONS. IF YOU DO NOT AGREE WITH THESE TERMS AND CONDITIONS, DO NOT INSTALL THE SOFTWARE AND RETURN THIS PACKAGE PROMPTLY FOR A FULL REFUND.

1. Grant of License
This software package is protected under United States copyright law and international treaty. You are hereby entitled to one copy of the enclosed software and are allowed by law to make one backup copy or to copy the contents of the disks onto a single hard disk and keep the originals as your backup or archival copy. United States copyright law prohibits you from making a copy of this software for use on any computer other than your own computer. United States copyright law also prohibits you from copying any written material included in this software package without first obtaining the permission of Adams Media Corporation.

2. Restrictions
You, the end-user, are hereby prohibited from the following:
You may not rent or lease the Software or make copies to rent or lease for profit or for any other purpose.
You may not disassemble or reverse compile for the purposes of reverse engineering the Software.
You may not modify or adapt the Software or documentation in whole or in part, including, but not limited to, translating or creating derivative works.

3. Transfer
You may transfer the Software to another person, provided that (a) you transfer all of the Software and documentation to the same transferee; (b) you do not retain any copies; and (c) the transferee is informed of and agrees to the terms and conditions of this Agreement.

4. Termination
This Agreement and your license to use the Software can be terminated without notice if you fail to comply with any of the provisions set forth in this Agreement. Upon termination of this Agreement, you promise to destroy all copies of the software including backup or archival copies as well as any documentation associated with the Software. All disclaimers of warranties and limitation of liability set forth in this Agreement shall survive any termination of this Agreement.

5. Limited Warranty
Adams Media Corporation warrants that the Software will perform according to the manual and other written materials accompanying the Software for a period of 30 days from the date of receipt. Adams Media Corporation does not accept responsibility for any malfunctioning computer hardware or any incompatibilities with existing or new computer hardware technology.

6. Customer Remedies
Adams Media Corporation's entire liability and your exclusive remedy shall be, at the option of Adams Media Corporation, either refund of your purchase price or repair and/or replacement of Software that does not meet this Limited Warranty. Proof of purchase shall be required. This Limited Warranty will be voided if Software failure was caused by abuse, neglect, accident or misapplication. All replacement Software will be warranted based on the remainder of the warranty or the full 30 days, whichever is shorter and will be subject to the terms of the Agreement.

7. No Other Warranties
ADAMS MEDIA CORPORATION, TO THE FULLEST EXTENT OF THE LAW, DISCLAIMS ALL OTHER WARRANTIES, OTHER THAN THE LIMITED WARRANTY IN PARAGRAPH 5, EITHER EXPRESS OR IMPLIED, ASSOCIATED WITH ITS SOFTWARE, INCLUDING BUT NOT LIMITED TO IMPLIED WARRANTIES OF MERCHANTABILITY AND FITNESS FOR A PARTICULAR PURPOSE, WITH REGARD TO THE SOFTWARE AND ITS ACCOMPANYING WRITTEN MATERIALS. THIS LIMITED WARRANTY GIVES YOU SPECIFIC LEGAL RIGHTS. DEPENDING UPON WHERE THIS SOFTWARE WAS PURCHASED, YOU MAY HAVE OTHER RIGHTS.

8. Limitations on Remedies
TO THE MAXIMUM EXTENT PERMITTED BY LAW, ADAMS MEDIA CORPORATION SHALL NOT BE HELD LIABLE FOR ANY DAMAGES WHATSOEVER, INCLUDING WITHOUT LIMITATION, ANY LOSS FROM PERSONAL INJURY, LOSS OF BUSINESS PROFITS, BUSINESS INTERRUPTION, BUSINESS INFORMATION OR ANY OTHER PECUNIARY LOSS ARISING OUT OF THE USE OF THIS SOFTWARE.
This applies even if Adams Media Corporation has been advised of the possibility of such damages. Adams Media Corporation's entire liability under any provision of this agreement shall be limited to the amount actually paid by you for the Software. Because some states may not allow for this type of limitation of liability, the above limitation may not apply to you.
THE WARRANTY AND REMEDIES SET FORTH ABOVE ARE EXCLUSIVE AND IN LIEU OF ALL OTHERS, ORAL OR WRITTEN, EXPRESS OR IMPLIED. No Adams Media Corporation dealer, distributor, agent, or employee is authorized to make any modification or addition to the warranty.

9. General
This Agreement shall be governed by the laws of the United States of America and the Commonwealth of Massachusetts. If you have any questions concerning this Agreement, contact Adams Media Corporation at 508-427-7100. Or write to us at: Adams Media Corporation, 57 Littlefield Street, Avon, MA 02322.